Harmony
and
Health

Love
and
Blessings

Christmas,
2006

Gordon

Translated from the French
Original title: «HARMONIE ET SANTÉ»

Original edition
© 1987, Éditions Prosveta S.A., France, ISBN 2-85566-428-4

© 1988, Éditions Prosveta S.A., France, ISBN 2-85566-443-8

Prosveta S.A – B.P.12 – 83601 Fréjus CEDEX (France)
ISBN 2-85566-443-8

Omraam Mikhaël Aïvanhov

Harmony and Health

Izvor Collection – No. 225

PROSVETA

Readers are asked to note that Omraam Mikhaël Aïvanhov's teaching was exclusively oral. This volume includes passages from several different lectures all dealing with the same theme.

TABLES OF CONTENTS

Chapter One

LIFE COMES FIRST

I

In the beginning is life. Look around you and observe the creatures of the earth: before anything else they have life, and only after that do they begin, to a greater or a lesser degree, to feel, think and act effectively.

Life! The word sums up all the undifferentiated, unorganized wealth of the universe before an organizing force disposes and apportions it and puts it to work. All future developments are potentially present in the word 'life'. As in a seed that needs only to be planted, watered and tended in order to produce fruit, a living cell already contains, potentially, all the future limbs and organs of the body. And just as, after a certain time, a tree begins to grow from a seed, so from this magma, from this chaos, from this indeterminate reality that is life, all this hidden potentiality gradually emerges and takes shape.

That is how the organs that we now possess first appeared, and many others will appear in the future. As our physical body is built in the image of our astral body, our astral body in the image of our mental body and so on, up to the divine plane, and as we have five sense organs on the physical plane (touch, taste, smell, hearing and sight), we also have five senses on the astral and mental planes. These subtle senses are not yet developed, but they are there, waiting to manifest themselves, and once they are fully formed, we shall have untold possibilities to see, hear, taste, act and move. Life, living beings, living cells, micro-organisms, contain in themselves all possibilities for their future development but it will be thousands of years before they manifest themselves fully. This is the mystery, the splendour of life!

Look at human beings: they come and go, work and play, and busy themselves with all kinds of things and, all the while, their life grows fainter and drains away because they don't care about it. They think that, since life has been given to them, they have a right to spend it to obtain all the other things they want: wealth, pleasure, knowledge or glory. So they draw on their reserves without restraint until, finding themselves bankrupt, they have to abandon all their activities. What a senseless way to behave! When we lose life we lose everything. The only thing that matters is life, and this means that we must protect, purify and sanctify it and eliminate whatever hinders it or gets in the way of its development, because life gives us health, strength, power, intelligence and beauty.

In my lecture about the wise and foolish virgins[1] I explained that the oil that Jesus spoke about symbolized life: when man has no more oil his lamp goes out and he dies. And in every domain you can find other symbols of life: for plants it is water; for the creatures who live on the surface of the earth it is air or, more specifically for human beings, blood; for commerce it is gold or silver; for a car it is petrol, and so on.

Life is the primeval matter, the reservoir from which new creations constantly emerge with ramifications stretching out to the infinite. And from this faceless, undifferentiated life which is no more than a potentiality, the spirit continues to create new elements and new forms.

But men and women are interested in everything except life. As a matter of fact, if life were their first priority, if they were really concerned to cherish and protect it and keep it absolutely pure, they would find more and more possibilities for obtaining all the other things they desire, because it is that enlightened, intense,

---

[1] See *New Light on the Gospels,* Izvor 217, chap. 9: 'The Parable of the Wise and Foolish Virgins'.

luminous life that can give them everything. But as this is alien to their philosophy, they fritter their life away in the belief that, just because they are alive, they have the right to do whatever they please with it. They all say, 'I'm alive and I mean to make the most of it!' but how many actually achieve what they set their sights on? Very few; most of them simply plunder their own resources. It is time to adopt a different philosophy, it is time to realize that your way of thinking has a direct effect on your life, on its reserves, on the very quintessence of your being, and that a wrong attitude distorts and damages everything.

Let me give you an example: take the case of a young man whose father is very rich. As long as he studies and works well his father gives him an allowance. But then, one day, the boy begins to get into trouble and wastes his father's money on amusements and, when his father responds by cutting off his allowance, he suddenly finds himself penniless! What is the boy's real fault in this case? The greatest possible fault: he has endangered his own life by cutting himself off from the conditions, energies and vital currents of which money is the symbol. And when we do the same thing by using and abusing our life as we please and allowing ourselves to break all the laws, we, too, exhaust our reserves and end by finding ourselves destitute: not materially, physically, destitute perhaps, but inwardly destitute. Life is the only wealth there is, and whatever we call it: money, subsidies, oil, quintessence, it comes to the same thing, for the word 'life' can be replaced by any of these terms.

Human beings squander their lives in the pursuit of all kinds of things that are less important than life itself. They work for years to achieve their ambitions and end by being so exhausted and jaded that, if you weigh up what they have gained against what they have lost, you will find that they have lost everything and gained very little. They are so constituted that they are ready to lose everything because they have never been taught that it is more important to have health and joy – even if one has nothing else – than to have great wealth and be incapable of enjoying it because one has worn oneself out running after it! There is a proverb that says, 'A living dog is better than a dead lion!' Yes, but there are a lot of people who would rather be dead lions!

What is lacking is the true philosophy. Human beings should be taught from their earliest childhood not to fritter away their life but to dedicate it to a sublime goal for, in that way, it becomes richer, stronger and more intense. Life is a capital which you can invest in a bank on high so that, instead of deteriorating and being wasted, its value increases

continually and, thanks to this wealth, you will
have the possibility of learning and working to
better purpose. Whereas, if you give yourself up to
pleasure, to your emotions and passions, you will
be throwing away your life, because everything
has to be paid for, and you will be paying with your
life! Nothing can be gained without the sacrifice of
something else. As the French say, 'You can't make
an omelette without breaking some eggs!' But I am
telling you that that is not true: you can make an
omelette without breaking eggs. I know the secret
of how to do it: put all your capital in a bank on
high and then, the more you work the stronger and
more powerful you will be. Yes, instead of growing
weaker and exhausting yourself, you will become
stronger because you will continually receive
new elements to replace those you spend. But, of
course, this will be true only if you place all your
'money', all your 'capital', in a heavenly bank!

This is why it is so important that you should
know whom you are working for and what goal
you are aiming at, for it is this that determines the
direction your energies will take. If, for instance,
you are working for your father – symbolically
speaking – you will not lose, you will gain. What
matters, therefore, is to know exactly what you are
spending your energies on, in what direction you
are working, for your future hangs on this: you are
getting either richer or poorer.

Without realizing it, most people work for an enemy within who is robbing and despoiling them. A true spiritualist[2] is more intelligent: the person he works and expends his energies for is his true self; it is he who gains. This is the intelligent thing to do: to know how to enrich oneself, not to become poorer. And this is not selfish; on the contrary, it is truly impersonal[3].

Suppose, for example, that you decide to work, not for yourself but for the collectivity. Yes, but you have ties with the collectivity, you are an integral part of it, and everything that improves and embellishes the collectivity improves and embellishes each individual member – including yourself. You gain because you have placed your capital in a bank called 'family', 'community', 'universal brotherhood', of which you are a mem-

---

[2] The word 'spiritualist', in the language of Omraam Mikhaël Aïvanhov, simply means one who looks at things from a spiritual point of view, whose philosophy of life is based on belief in a spiritual reality.

[3] This use of the word 'impersonal' may be misunderstood if it is not placed in the context of Omraam Mikhaël Aïvanhov's teaching concerning the two natures in man, the human and the divine, the lower self and the higher Self or, as he terms them, the personality and the individuality. For a fuller treatment of the subject, see *The Key to the Problems of Existence* C.W. 11, and *Man's Two Natures, Human and Divine*, Izvor 213.

ber. If you decide to work for yourself, on the other hand, for your own mediocre little 'self', your energies will be wasted and do you no good at all. You will object, 'That can't be true. I'll certainly gain from all that work I'm doing for myself!' No. That is where you are mistaken, for your personal, separate, egotistical self is a bottomless pit, and by working for it you throw everything into that pit. That is not how you should work! Those who are too individualistic and selfish have no notion of what they might gain if they worked for the collectivity. They say, 'I'm no fool. I'm working for myself and I'm getting on nicely...' and that is precisely how they lose all their capital.

When I speak of 'the collectivity', I am not speaking only of mankind, but of the whole universe, of all creatures in the universe and even of God Himself. This Universal Collectivity, this Immensity for which you are working, is like a bank, and all the work you do for it will be paid back to you many times over. For the universe runs a very prosperous business! It is continually acquiring new constellations, new nebulae, new galaxies and, one day, all this wealth will be yours.

Those who work for themselves instead of for the whole, impoverish themselves, and nobody remembers or loves them, not even their own family, for they are far too egocentric. They never think of others, so why should others think of them? They end their lives in disappointment, bitterness and grief. You might think that it would occur to them that it was their own philosophy of life that was at fault, but no, not a bit of it! They have always been in the right and everybody else is wicked and unjust! They deserve to be loved and helped! 'Deserve, deserve!' But what have they ever done to deserve anything good? Those who are full of love, kindness and self-denial may be considered ridiculous to begin with, and people may exploit and take advantage of them for a time, but they will gradually be recognized and loved for what they are: truly exceptional human beings. And then they will be cherished and rewarded. They work for the good of the universe and, one day, they will get their reward. But not at once, of course.

When you put money into a bank you don't receive the interest on it the very next day. You have to wait, and the longer you wait the more interest you get. The same law applies in the spiritual domain. You may have been working with much love, patience and faith and to begin with you see no results. But don't be discouraged; if you give way to discouragement it shows that you have not understood the laws that govern your daily life. Yes, you have to know the rules of banking and administration! If you knew them you would realize that one always has to wait. In the long run, riches will rain down on you from all sides; the whole universe will fling fabulous wealth at you. In fact, even if you wanted to avoid your reward it would be impossible: you will have brought it all on yourself. It is only fair!

So you can see how short-sighted an egocentric philosophy is. People rely on appearances, but appearances lie – how often I have told you this! If you want to discover the truth you will have to look beyond appearances; that which seems to be useful and advantageous for today is very often harmful for the future.

So, never waste or barter your life for the sake of anything else, for nothing has greater value than life. Obviously, there are a few exceptional cases in which men have given their lives in order to save others or in defence of an ideal. The Prophets and Initiates, who gave their lives for an ideal or for the glory of God, did not, in fact, lose anything, for Heaven gave them a new, far richer, far more beautiful life, to reward them for having sacrificed their earthly life for the cause of good. So I am not saying that one must always, and in every case, preserve one's life: there are rare exceptions. But generally speaking a disciple has a duty to preserve, purify and intensify his life because life is the source, the reservoir, the starting point for every other development, whether on the intellectual, religious, emotional, aesthetic or any other plane.

You will perhaps disagree with me when I say that human beings do not value life or work to preserve it, and protest that, on the contrary, everybody is anxious to prolong life. To prolong it, yes, I agree, but not to spiritualize and purify it or to illuminate and sanctify it and make it divine. People want to prolong their lives because they want to continue their pursuit of pleasure, their crimes and their shady business deals. Do you really believe that doctors want to prolong human lives so that they may be dedicated to the service of Light or the good of the world? Not at all: it is perfectly true when I say that no one really cares about life: no one cares about true life. In other words, no one is capable of obtaining joy, beauty, power, wealth, renown or knowledge without making a mess of his life. In one way or another, whatever people do, they always manage to make a mess of their lives!

When you decide to work exclusively for the embellishment, intensification, purification and sanctification of your life, all your faculties are enhanced because that pure, harmonious life reaches out to other regions and other beings and they come to help and inspire you. Indirectly, therefore, it is life that obtains all the rest for you, but only if it is pure and harmonious.

The day you understand that the way you live is what matters, you will receive all that you have

ever wished for without having to ask for it. That
is so true, in fact, that I feel like saying exactly the
opposite of Jesus: '*Don't* ask and you will receive;
don't seek and you will find; *don't* knock and it
will be opened to you!' Yes, but when is this true?
When you live a divine life. There, now you know!
And one day this will be written in the new Gospel,
for Jesus thought this too, but he could not say it.
The people of his day would not have understood.
If he came back today, he would say, 'Live a divine
life, ask for nothing and you will have everything!'
Why? Because when you live a divine life you are
giving, and he who gives receives. And even if you
have never expressed any special desire it does not
matter, Heaven will shower you with blessings.

II

The day you discover how to emanate life in such a way that it reveals everything and opens all doors to you, you will at last know what life really is. From now on, therefore, you must do everything possible to intensify the life within you and make it fruitful, for it is capable of working the highest magic in hearts and souls and minds, in the entities and forces of nature and even on physical objects. Yes, it is time you understood how idiotic it is to throw away an eternity of splendour for the sake of a paltry existence spent in eating and drinking, sleeping and running round in all directions, trying to satisfy one's vilest appetites! Tell me, do you really think that this is an intelligent way to behave?

If Initiates are well-balanced and full of peace and every other blessing, it is because they have understood that the most potent form of magic is found in life and nowhere else. Yes, in life; in being capable of breathing life into others. There is no greater magic than that of animating and stimulating human beings, of firing them with enthusiasm and resuscitating them. Anyone who does not understand this is destroying the very roots of his existence. He will never know what true life is!

Why do you eat three or even four times a day? You eat and drink and then you go to work, or read a book, etc. But why do you start by eating? While you eat, are you learning something? Are you working? No, but you are imbibing life, and when life gets into you it irrigates every cell in your arms and legs, your ears, mouth, brain etc., and gives them energy. Then your legs can run and win you the first prize in a race; your arms can flail like windmills so that you become a boxing champion and win all the trophies, and your tongue can start rattling away like a machine gun... and win even more victories! And so on with your ears, your brain... every bit of you. But if you don't eat, you will not be able to run or to box or even to talk. So, you see, once you have introduced life into your organism, it sees to it that all your cells are vivified, strengthened and stimulated so that all your faculties become active. The foundation, therefore, is life: it is life that animates and nourishes all the rest.

Similarly, as I have discovered from observing what goes on in our daily lives, life can put us in touch with the divine world. I am inventing nothing; if you cannot see this, it is because you are not observant. If your eyes can see and your ears hear, it is because you have eaten. Try going without food for a few days and you will neither see nor hear quite so well. When life flags everything else flags, whereas, when you manage to make your life luminous, pure and spiritual, it opens other ears and eyes within you, and you begin to hear and see invisible realities: laws, truths and correspondences. True Initiates do not learn these things from books; they see and hear the subtle realities of the invisible world which are still unknown to philosophers and scientists. And they are able to do so because they possess this higher form of life which animates their subtle bodies. It is life itself which gives them these revelations, so the great thing is to possess that life.

Some of you will say, 'But I'm very much alive! I can eat and drink and go about my business.' Perhaps, but you are not really alive, you are content with the life of a vegetable; you don't know what it means to be really alive. For there are different degrees of life: billions of different degrees. This is why Jesus said, *'I have come that they may have life, and that they may have it more abundantly'*. What life was he speaking about?

Surely his disciples were already alive? Yes, but Jesus spoke of another kind of life, a degree of life so subtle, spiritual, luminous and divine that it enables man to see, hear, feel, taste and touch a reality which is beyond the reach of a purely physical, animal life. This is what Jesus understood by 'life', and he prayed that Heaven would give his disciples that life, the only kind of life which enables man to understand and breathe freely in the Heavenly regions.

You all know the words of the Master Peter Deunov's song: *'Sine moi pazi jivota'*: 'My son, keep your life safe; this treasure deep within you...' This shows that the Master Peter Deunov had this same understanding of the importance of life. Yes, and now we need teachers and pedagogues capable of throwing light on this essential question of life.

You sow a seed and it becomes a tree with roots, a trunk, branches, leaves, flowers and fruit. How did the seed manage to produce all that wealth? It was life that did it. Life possesses every possibility in itself, but it has to be channelled in the right direction just like water. If you don't lay your pipes so that the water reaches the fruit and vegetables in your garden it will not do them any good and they will die. But a gardener knows this: he digs his ditches and lays his pipes in advance and then the water flows along them and waters all his plants. Why have you never thought about this? It would help you to understand that the first thing to work at is life; in other words, to find water and then to pump it to where it is needed. And a human being, like a skyscraper of twenty, fifty or a hundred floors, needs water at the highest levels.

Yes, a human being is like a skyscraper, not with a mere hundred and fifty floors, but with thousands of floors, and he has to pump water to the inhabitants of all those floors, all the way to the very top floor, the brain. But what do most of them do? Instead of irrigating their spiritual cells, they let it all run down to the lower levels where their instincts, passions and lowest desires live, and then they have none left for the top storeys. The inhabitants on their top floors are always so somnolent, numb and paralysed that they are incapable of doing anything productive. Yes, there are entities in the brain whose work is to do research, make observations, emit and receive messages, but the lack of 'water' makes them too anaemic to work properly and carry out their functions.

If man does not evolve as he should, it is because he never thinks of orientating his life towards the sublime regions. Life is that which blossoms and bears fruit. Not long after you have sown a seed, life begins to manifest itself. Its

language is easily recognizable: the appearance
of tiny rootlets, shoots, leaves and buds. Life is
an embellishment, an enrichment, an overflowing,
and if you begin to care for your own life, if you
plant and water it, if you train it to grow upwards
it will flourish and, in flourishing, it will awaken
cells and faculties within you whose existence you
have never even suspected.

As you can see, nutrition explains everything.
When you eat you take in life and, if you steer it
in the right direction, that life infiltrates into every
corner of your being, bringing you joy and states
of consciousness of untold richness and splendour.
Even poets and musicians are incapable of doing
justice to all the forms, colours, expressions and
melodies by which life manifests itself.

But then the question arises: 'How is it that no
one, not even biologists, know what life is?' They
know a great many things, they can explain all
kinds of chemical combinations, but when it comes
to life, all they can say is that it is the greatest of
all mysteries. Yes, life is such a mystery to them
because it has never occurred to them that they
must move onto a much higher level if they want to
find out what it is. Life can only be known above,
not below. On the lower level are the vital instincts,
animal, vegetable and mineral life. But when
human beings climb to the sublime heights from
which life originates, when they have acquired

much subtler, much more spiritual perceptions, then they will discover what it really is.

Life is God Himself. There is no life outside of God. It is He who creates and distributes it and, if men are incapable of knowing life, it is because their consciousness is no longer in touch with God. God is the source of life; only those who turn back to the Godhead can know life. Only God creates life and only He can teach us the mystery of life.

Today, for the very first time, try to understand me. Make up your minds to say, 'Yes, we are going to change the direction of our lives, to harmonize them and make them fruitful, to consecrate and sanctify them.' If you do this, everything will begin to change for the better, including your health and your self-perception, and whatever comes your way after this will be of a different nature. But if you cling stubbornly to your old conceptions it will be your loss; you will continue to rub along for a few more years and then, when you get to the other side, you will be shown what a beggarly, pitiful existence you have led. Even if you have devoured whole libraries full of books, even if you have five or six university degrees, you will still be told that you have lived like an animal and delayed your evolution tremendously.

I have already said this: what is important is your goal, the ideal for which you are working. That is all that matters. Stop thinking that you have to live and think in such and such a way in order to meet with the approval of your fellow men, that is not true life; it is only a pretence. Make an effort to live a divine life like those who are unafraid, bold and persevering enough to keep going in spite of obstacles and adversity and, one day, you will be given strength, power and light.

Obviously, those who prefer the pretence will always find a few crusts to gnaw on, but what a tragic future they are laying up for themselves! They don't realize that they, in turn, are being gnawed to the bone by other entities. Whereas those who are not seduced by appearances and have chosen authentic reality could tell you of the riches and glories in which they live. These are the ones you should be listening to; trust them, follow them; don't be content to stick to the beaten track. It may seem safer, of course, since everybody goes that way, and the narrow paths that lead to the peak may be more dangerous. But that is not a valid argument!

Life is the water that nourishes and vivifies and, if you send it upwards and nourish all those anaemic, somnolent beings in your upper storeys with it, they will wake up and begin working again and, thanks to the delicate instruments in their possession, they will give you all the information you need about the universe and your own inner life. Is there any need for me to give you examples

of how people waste their life? Take the question
of love, for instance: so many people fritter away
their love in the dust below instead of sending it up
to nourish the entities in their brain. And the result
is that they lose all their inner light and become
more and more like animals, because their lives
are turned in the direction of the abyss. Whereas
others, who have consecrated that energy and who
try to sublimate and transform it, become geniuses
and teachers and benefactors of humanity.

If you have understood me correctly today you
are in a position to rebuild your future. Make up
your minds, at last, to vivify those beings that dwell
in you so that they can do their work. So far, you
have not known how to interpret the phenomena
that take place before your eyes every day; you
have never realized that exactly the same patterns
exist in the spiritual domain. And, above all, you
have never understood that life is the only true
magic, that it is life that is capable of winning you
the admiration, love and respect of men and of the
whole universe. If you want to practise magic you
can: no need to pronounce strange formulas or draw
circles around yourself, no need for fumigations or
mysterious ceremonies. Concentrate on improving
and enhancing your life, enrich it with ever more
love, selflessness and purity and then distribute it,
scatter it abroad throughout the length and breadth
of the universe.

From now on, accept what I tell you and stop wasting your life. Perhaps you will ask, 'But are you telling us that we shouldn't work to earn money and have a house and a car, or get married and have children?' No, I have never said that. I am simply saying that most people go to such extremes in these things that they destroy themselves. It is quite enough to work sufficiently to provide for your material needs and still leave yourself time to think, meditate and love. Why be so set on having everything? People want first one thing and then another and then yet another... and play havoc with their lives in attempting to get what they want. No, you must work reasonably and dedicate your work to a divine idea. All those people who want to get to the top of the tree and be president or chairman or champion of this, that or the other, are obliged to push themselves beyond certain limits, with the result, of course, that they destroy their physical and emotional balance and end up in hospital or a psychiatric clinic! And yet these are the people everybody looks up to and tries to imitate!

As for young people, their models are film stars, pop singers, mobsters, drug addicts or anarchists, and they are ready to go to any lengths to be like them. The media – press, films, plays and advertising – all urge them to follow this pernicious path. It is as though they had sworn to bring about the downfall of mankind – and their own downfall, at the same time, of course! Human beings are rushing headlong towards the abyss but, as they cannot see it, they are unwilling even to admit that it exists and continue on their mad course. If they could see the chasm yawning at their feet they might be more careful, but as it is still far off and well camouflaged, they race on and on. But there comes a time when, even though they can see the danger before them, they are unable to stop or change course and they fall over the edge. Time and again people have said to me: 'I can see the open pit at my feet but I can't stop!'

And now, if you ask me why there are so few who decide to change their life and the way they think, feel and behave, I will say that the first reason is that they have no clear idea of the advantages to be gained from such a change. They are persuaded that the kind of life that every Tom, Dick and Harry leads is true life. People are always saying, 'That's life!' Yes, when something goes wrong, whenever something really sad or terrible happens, they say, 'Well, what can you expect? That's life!' How can they be expected to change if they don't believe that there is a better kind of life to be had? Secondly, nobody thinks that it is possible to change. And thirdly, for most people, it is extremely difficult to change, it demands too much of them, so they never really make up their minds to attempt it.

Everything else is easy by comparison: to get a degree or earn a lot of money is easy, but to change one's life and transform oneself, that is another matter entirely!

To be sure, scientists are looking for ways to improve the human race, but their work is restricted to the physical plane. They think that if they can change human chromosomes they will be able to produce geniuses. Perhaps. But that is another question; it does not alter the fact that it is very difficult to change. On the other hand, I have already given you quantities of methods that you can use to change your life and transform yourselves. Take the method of grafting, for example: suppose you have a quince tree in your garden which produces only hard, sour fruit: you can put all that vigour to good use and get it to produce juicy, succulent fruit by making just a few grafts. Of course, as I have already explained, you must understand that I am talking about inner, psychic grafts[4].

In point of fact it is not really so terribly hard to transform oneself; it all depends on how much you really want to do so. When you are sick and tired of yourself to the point of nausea, and your desire to transform and improve yourself becomes really intense, it can produce a quite extraordinary effect.

---

[4] See *True Alchemy or the Quest for Perfection,* Izvor 221, chap. 7: 'Grafting'.

But the question is: do people feel this intense desire? Perhaps they do but it never lasts long; they abandon it after a day or two, and all their good resolutions come to nothing. You must nourish this desire constantly and, one day, everything will change, you will be completely transformed... Yes, and this is the resurrection! Most people imagine that they must wait until the end of time for the resurrection, for the day when all the dead awake and come out of their graves; that is how Christians understand these things! What a splendid sight that would be: all those dead people getting up and walking about! No, no; it is here and now, in this life, that we have to rise from the dead.

Chapter Two

THE WORLD OF HARMONY

In choosing to talk to you about harmony I realize that it is going to be very difficult for you to understand me, not intellectually, of course, but in depth, with your whole being, for this is not a subject that interests human beings particularly. On the contrary, their way of life involves them in occupations and activities that are far removed from harmony, especially from harmony as the Initiates conceive it! But still, try to listen attentively to what I have to say.

If you are really concerned about your own perfection, about fulfilment and final victory, you must work for harmony. That is to say, you must try to harmonize your being with all the forces of the universe. The power of a spiritualist resides, precisely, in his will to be in harmony with the body of the universe, to climb to the highest summit and live with the life of God Himself.

A world of harmony exists, an eternal world from which has come the infinite variety of forms, colours, sounds, perfumes and flavours that we know. Years ago, Heaven gave me the privilege of tasting this perfect harmony: I was snatched from my body and permitted to hear the Harmony of the Spheres. Never have I known anything to equal the intensity and richness of the sensations I experienced. There is nothing I can compare it to; it was indescribable, almost unbearable, so strongly did I feel that I was being stretched and diluted in space. It was so beautiful, so divine that I was afraid; I was afraid of that splendour, for I felt my whole being expanding to such an extent that I was in danger of dissolving and disintegrating into space. So I cut short the ecstasy and came back to earth. Now, I regret it, of course! But at least, for a few seconds, I actually experienced it, I actually saw and heard the whole universe vibrating. Rocks, trees, mountains, the oceans and stars, the suns and every creature sang together in such magnificent, sublime harmony, it was as though... But, no! It cannot be compared to anything in the physical world. And I was afraid! Yes, it was so powerful, so intense, only a few seconds more and I would have been dead, blown to dust! Heaven gave me the privilege of that experience so that I should have some idea of what Heavenly harmony really is. Pythagoras and Plato and many other philosophers have talked about this harmony, but I wonder how many of them actually experienced it.

And today the memory of that experience is enough to fill my soul, as though nothing else were needed to sustain, strengthen and nourish my spiritual life. Yes, it is enough to know how the universe is put together; to know how it all vibrates in harmony, in accordance with the will of Cosmic Intelligence, from whom every object and every living being has received its own particular note, its own voice.

I have often heard people expressing astonishment at the unity that characterizes all the lectures I have given you over the years; it is as though everything I said flowed from one central source, for nothing I say ever contradicts what I have said before. Yes, and let me tell you that it is not because of any books I have read that I am able to see this unity so clearly, but because I have heard the Music of the Spheres. In the presence of that harmony one understands the structure and destination of the universe and how it lives and vibrates. People believe that one has to read books to learn the secrets of creation, that it takes long years of study to discover truth. No, if you want to know truth, you must look to the world above, not to the world below. For years, I practised astral projection in order to study that construction, that organization that we call the cosmos. And I succeeded: I succeeded in contemplating the universe, not as we see it with our eyes, clothed in flesh and blood, but as a structure in the world of archetypes. When I heard the Harmony of the Spheres it was the crowning point of all my research, all my work, all my out-of-body experiences. And, ever since, it has remained as a criterion, an example, a touchstone, a model which enables me to understand and recognize how everything else fits in.

Well, now you know that I draw everything I tell you in my lectures from the region in which I heard the Heavenly Harmony, the Music of the Spheres. It is this that explains everything to me, although, if the truth be told, there is not really so much that needs to be explained. All one has to do is to achieve this harmony and, in an instant, everything becomes clear and one understands God's wisdom, one understands peace, one understands love. How often some of you have said to me, 'Yesterday I understood everything! And today I understand nothing!' The reason is that you have disrupted your inner harmony. This is why you must constantly soak yourselves in the word 'harmony' night and day. Think of nothing else. Keep it in your mind as a kind of pitch-pipe: as soon as you feel slightly upset or off-key, listen to it and tune your whole being to the region of harmony.

Yes, for this region really does exist; Cabbalists mention it in their explanations of the Tree of Life, the Sephirotic Tree. Each Sephirah of the

Tree of Life expresses a particular nuance of divine harmony, but the Sephirah that presides over the Harmony of the Spheres is *Chokmah*, and the name of God in this Sephirah is *Yah*. His servant is *Raziel*, Archangel of light, knowledge and wisdom and of the power of the Divine Word. *Raziel* commands the *Ophanim* (Christian tradition knows them as the Cherubim) who, under the authority of the Word, watch over the harmony of the cosmos. Their empire is immense, stretching all the way to the Zodiac, of which the Hebrew name is Mazloth.

If you are seeking your own happiness and fulfilment you must think about harmony and work to bring yourself into harmony with the whole universe. If you persevere at this, the day will come when you will feel that your whole being, from the tips of your toes to the top of your head, is in communion and vibrating in unison with Cosmic Life. When this moment comes – not before – you will understand what life, creation and love are; before that, it is not possible to understand. Intellectually, outwardly, you may imagine that you have understood, but it is not possible: genuine understanding cannot be achieved thanks to the work of a few brain cells. It is the whole being, the whole body that must understand: even your feet, your arms, your stomach and liver... True understanding involves every cell of your body.

Understanding is a sensation: you feel something
and then you know and understand it because you
have felt and tasted it.

No amount of intellectual understanding can
compare to the understanding of sensation. When
you experience love, hatred, anger or sorrow, you
know what it is. If you say that you know what
love is, without ever having been in love, you are
lying! But if you have truly experienced love, then
you know what it is. You may be unable to explain
or express it, but you know it; you really and truly
know it. Knowledge is to vibrate in unison with
all that exists. When your whole body vibrates in
unison with a truth, a sensation or an object, you
know that truth, sensation or object. This is why
the essential preoccupation of a disciple must be
to attune himself to the Heavenly Hierarchies so as
to vibrate in unison with them. If he works for this
harmony night and day, he will, one day, experience
sensations beautiful and precious beyond words.
Whereas he who propagates disorder will, one
day, be ground to dust and destroyed because he is
working with negative, hostile, destructive forces.
Once and for all, you must make up your minds
to get to know the laws of Nature, but also to get
to know the structure of man and how he should
relate to those laws.

When you manage to touch someone's heart,
you touch his whole being. If you touch only his

feet, his fingers or an ear, it will not have much effect. But touch his heart, and his whole being begins to feel involved. If you have been deeply moved by someone, you say, 'He spoke to my heart'. So we must touch the heart: the heart of other beings, the heart of things, the heart of the universe. And you can only touch the heart of the universe by means of harmony. Thanks to harmony you will attract all the other virtues and qualities; they will flock to you because you have touched the heart and not just the outskirts, the fringe.

But don't think that you can touch the heart of the universe with your insignificant little qualities. It does not make much difference whether you are avaricious or generous, highly-strung or placid, compassionate or hard-hearted. There are many very virtuous people who have never succeeded in touching the heart of the Eternal Father. You can only touch His heart by being in harmony with Him, by vibrating in unison with Him. You all choose just one modest little quality or virtue to cultivate: patience, tolerance, generosity, etc. Oh, they are all right, I admit; but they are only scraps compared to the immensity of harmony. Obviously, it is excellent to be generous, kind, indulgent, gentle and humble; but there are a lot of people who still live in disharmony in spite of all these virtues; they are not enough to make them perfect. So you would do better to leave them alone; don't

bother about them any more! You are horrified,
aren't you? 'But that's a terrible thing to say! How
can you give such bad advice? Religion has never
taught anything like that!' No, but you would do
much better to leave religion alone, too! Take care
of this one thing: harmony, and it will take care of
all the other virtues.

If you work to introduce harmony into your
whole being, to live in it and propagate it to all
around you, there will be no need for you to work
at each particular virtue or quality. For the first time
I am telling you that you should not try to develop
one particular virtue, because it takes much too
long. A whole life-time would probably not be
enough, and, while you are working at one virtue,
what would you do about all the others? Your
whole life would be spent in becoming patient, or
tolerant or gentle, and all the other qualities would
be neglected.

So, I repeat: don't focus on this or that virtue
in particular. Concentrate only on harmony and,
at one stroke, it will cause all the other virtues
to blossom, too. This is what I do: I leave all the
other virtues alone. I make no attempt to become
generous or patient or indulgent; it is simply not
worthwhile, it would be a waste of time. I am
interested only in living in harmony and I have
seen for myself that this enables me to manifest
all the other virtues as well, for harmony forces

me to be intelligent and wise and understanding. Just try being wise or kind when your inner life is in turmoil: you will not succeed! And for no other reason than your appalling state of inner confusion and disharmony.

All this should give you plenty of matter for reflection. Harmonize everything within you and you will become capable of acting with such wisdom, perspicacity and intelligence that you will wonder in astonishment where it all comes from! Yes, if you are guided by harmony you will be capable of unravelling all kinds of difficult situations and of helping others by finding solutions and giving good advice. Shun disharmony as your worst enemy for, once it gets a grip on you, it will ravage and destroy you and there is no virtue capable of saving you.

Harmony, you see, is the synthesis of all qualities and virtues. When you cultivate harmony you touch the heart of reality, the Universal Soul, the Centre. And from this central core come the orders and the currents and forces that transform and organize everything. When you are not in a state of harmony, when you are upset, irritable or tense, you may make heroic efforts to manifest at least one virtue, but it will be to no avail. All that is bad and destructive in you rises to the surface to bite and sting and kick and destroy. However hard you try you will never make much

progress if you have forgotten the mother of all
qualities and virtues: harmony. When you are in
a state of harmony, everything in you blossoms:
the expression of your eyes and face are more
beautiful, your gestures are measured and more
graceful, your words more constructive, your
thoughts more intelligent. It is said that sloth is the
mother of all vices; but nobody ever speaks of the
mother of all virtues which is harmony.

Musicians, of course, can talk about harmony;
in fact you would be astonished at the wealth of
their explanations. But they cannot reveal the
Initiatic aspect of harmony to you, because they
do not know it themselves. From a strictly musical
point of view, they have a lot to teach, but no
musician is capable of telling you the things I have
just told you about harmony: the fact that harmony
is related to every virtue, to perfection and even
to health. Yes, even to health, for the least sign of
disharmony undermines and erodes one's health.
He who understands this will have only one desire:
to attune himself to the Entities and Intelligences
of the divine world, to create harmony within every
cell of his being.

Only harmony can unlock for us all the precious
gifts and blessings of Heaven, for Heaven responds
only to the language of harmony. If you want to
talk to Heaven, to beg for a favour or for protection,
you must realize that there is no other language.

You can rant and rave (and even threaten never to go church again if you don't get what you want!), but it will make no difference: Heaven will remain unmoved. But if you speak the language of music, by which I mean the language of harmony which is absolute music, music itself, music *par excellence*, then Heaven will hear you and answer your prayer. There is only one language spoken in Heaven, the language of harmony, and if you are capable of speaking to Heaven in that language, it will respond by sending you everything in abundance.

I can see that you make strenuous efforts in all kinds of areas, in the belief that they are more important and that they will shelter and protect you and bring you happiness. And, in the meantime, you neglect harmony. But perhaps you will understand me better today for, as I have pointed out, it is in your own interest; it is very much to your advantage to work ceaselessly and untiringly to achieve harmony, for it is the only thing that can give you all the other things you long for: friendship, love and, above all, the divine presence. It has often happened that, when we have been singing together, our singing has brought us closer to the realm of perfect harmony and you have felt the presence of heavenly entities amongst us. This is what attracts them: the harmony. They come amongst us, distributing flowers and gifts, and you sense their presence, but without realizing

what it is you are feeling. Continue to make
every effort, to do everything in your power until
Heaven yields and comes amongst us; and I assure
you: It will come. It is already with us, in fact;
It is behind all our efforts and, one day, you will
witness marvellous manifestations. When that day
comes you will be filled with such joy that you will
be unable to contain it all. You will be flooded by
currents so powerful that you will throb and vibrate
in purest ecstasy.

Harmony is the corner-stone of all success, of
every divine realization. It must be your constant
preoccupation to introduce harmony into your
being; only on this condition can you begin to
accomplish certain tasks which will bear fruit
for eternity. A tremendous amount of work and
tremendous strength of mind and concentration
are needed to achieve this harmony! But once
one has achieved it, prodigious forces are at one's
command for the good of mankind. Can't you feel
that the whole universe, all the forces of nature,
agree with what I am saying? Just take a good,
hard look and you will see that the whole of nature
confirms and endorses my words.

Every day, you must make an effort to vibrate
in harmony with the whole of creation. Begin by
establishing harmony between yourself and God,
the Creative Principle and First Cause. Say to Him:
'My God, I have always been foolish and ignorant,

but now I recognize my faults and am ready to do better: please forgive me. From now on I want to be in harmony with You. Give me Your light that I may no longer break Your laws. Allow me to contemplate You. I promise to obey You and do Your will.'

Next, you turn to the Angels and Archangels and say: 'Holy Angels, so often, when you have brought messages from the Creator to warn or enlighten me, I was deafened by the tumult of my passions and unable to hear your voice. I beseech you to continue to send me light, for I want to obey you. I know that you are the Lord's most exalted servants: I respect and love you.'

After this you can speak to the Masters and benefactors of mankind, to all those who have made the ultimate sacrifice for the Divine Cause: 'Oh, Masters of Mankind, I have never listened to you because I valued human knowledge above all else. But now I know that what you have discovered and understood is the only essential Truth and I want to help and serve you. Send me some of your learning and knowledge.'

Next, establish harmony between yourself and your fellow men: 'Beloved brothers and sisters, may peace and harmony reign in our midst! Let us forget each other's faults and failings; let us forget the evil we may have done to each other, and work side by side in the Lord's fields so as to transform the earth into a Garden of Paradise in which we may all live as brothers.'

Speak, also, to the animals: 'When God first created the world, you lived in peace and harmony with man; we owe you some help because it is by our fault that you have become cruel and have to survive under such difficult conditions. I send you light to help you advance rapidly on the path of evolution.'

Speak to plants: 'Oh lovely plants, flowers and trees; you who are willing to stay still and submit to all weathers, what a wonderful example you give us! Thank you for nourishing us; thank you for the beauty and fragrance of your flowers. I send you thoughts of love, I want to be in harmony with you. Give me your freshness and purity in return for my love.'

Speak to the stones of the earth: 'Oh you who bear the weight of humanity, you who give us the ground under our feet and the inspiring example of your age-old stability, you who give us materials for our houses and all kinds of beautiful buildings, give us also your strength, and we in turn shall give you ours so that, one day, you may awaken to consciousness. May there be harmony henceforth between us!'

Close your eyes and say to the whole universe: 'I love you, I love you, I love you! I am in harmony with you!'

Chapter Three

HARMONY AND HEALTH

In wanting to be independent and to free themselves from the Lord, human beings repeat the sin of Lucifer and our first parents by opposing His will and putting obstacles in the way of His plans. This desire to liberate oneself, to be anarchic, to defy God's orders, is the cause of all the misfortunes of mankind. You simply must understand this. It is very simple and clear and can be said in a few words: the day men broke the bonds that linked them to Heavenly harmony, misfortune began to rain down on them. And things are bound to go from bad to worse, for men are moving ceaselessly further and further from God, becoming more and more lawless and anarchic; they have no respect for anything any more. Yes, all this is reaching terrifying proportions. Wherever you look, even amongst the members of organized religions and spiritual teachings... all are infected with the germ of anarchy. We had better prepare ourselves for the disasters that lie ahead: wars, disease, etc.

But there is another thing that it is important to understand, and that is that the more the spirit of anarchy prevails in the world, the more cancer there will be. Every organic disease results from a weakness or vice in the individual; it is human beings who create their own illnesses. When nervous tension is too strong, one kind of illness appears; excessive sensuality produces another kind of illness; when disharmony increases, yet another kind of illness appears. Every illness is the result of a certain disorder, and cancer is the specific result of anarchy. To guard against it, therefore, we have to work at harmony, to think about harmony every day, to ensure that we are in harmony with the whole of mankind, the whole universe. Of course, I know that no one is capable of living perpetually in a state of perfect harmony, but you can always be conscious and vigilant, so that, as soon as you realize that you have slipped back into disharmony, you can get a grip on yourself and reverse the situation again. You must never allow yourself to harbour a climate of disharmony for long, for it will spread into all your cells and your organism will find it more and more difficult to resist the disorder it creates.

To be sure, each organ of our body has its own specialization and concentrates on doing its own work without bothering about what the others are doing. You cannot expect every organ to be concerned about what is happening in the rest of the body. In order to ensure harmony and the good of the whole, therefore, the Cosmic Spirit has put a higher intelligence in charge, and thanks to this higher intelligence in man, the functions of each organ are regulated and their specialization is used and directed for the benefit of the whole body.

A human being is placed between his own physical organs and the intelligence he has received from Heaven. If he gives priority to certain organs, the stomach or sexual organs for instance, and forgets about the whole, anarchy gets a hold on him and he begins to deteriorate. But if he gives priority to the balanced rule of intelligence, then he experiences a state of harmony which makes him capable of working and creating without ceasing.

Unfortunately, today, there is a growing spirit of anarchy abroad in the world. It is almost as though there were schools in which people learned to disrupt society by inciting others to anger and a spirit of revolt. The forces of darkness are at work, it is they that are responsible for this diabolical work. Some countries, instead of propagating the viruses of disease – because this would bring condemnation from all the other countries – have chosen to destroy their enemies by propagating the virus of discontent and revolt. And there you have cancer! All the anarchists and rebels against society are unwitting carriers of the disease. The Initiatic orders, on the other hand, which work for the reign of peace, harmony and brotherhood so that all men may come to understand, love and be united with their fellows, are propagating antibodies that destroy the germs of cancer. If these Initiatic centres did not exist, the whole of humanity would have been contaminated a long time ago. I know that very few people will accept this notion. They will say, 'What on earth is he talking about? There is no connection between anarchy and cancer. No biologist thinks so, anyway!' Well, if they want to stick with the opinion of biologists, that is their business! But I tell you that cancer is the result of the widespread anarchy in the world today. This is the truth, and this is why we must work ceaselessly to restore harmony.

Unfortunately, compared to the vast numbers of those who work for destruction and create mountains of difficulty and obscurity, there is no more than a handful of human beings in the world who understand that we must unite and work in harmony in order to counteract the ills that threaten humanity: war, poverty and disease. This tiny minority is not mighty enough to combat the evil influence of the majority for, to achieve anything on earth, numbers are extremely important: the numbers of those who are good, pure and enlightened and capable of taking part in the formation of a universal brotherhood whose decisions would have some weight in world affairs. Instead of understanding and uniting in order to transform the world, instead of collaborating in this tremendous work, most human beings choose to be individualistic and work only for their own interests.

A true spiritualist, on the contrary, works for a divine idea and it is this idea that sustains and rewards him. Yes, for it is directly linked to Heaven; it is a world in itself and it takes upon itself to fill him with joy, enthusiasm and hope. If you do not work for a divine idea, even if your other activities bring in a lot of money, you will not possess joy or happiness because you will not have this link with Heaven. But if you work for a divine idea, even if no one ever says thank you or acknowledges what you do, you will always feel fulfilled. It is important that you should understand this. Anchor a divine idea in your head, work for a divine idea, and you will see what that idea can do for you: it will improve your whole existence, it will even prolong your life!

Try to understand the power and efficacy of an idea, to understand how active and alive it is! Believe me, nothing is more potent or more stimulating than a divine idea! I tell you this because I have experienced it for myself. In fact, everything I tell you is drawn from my own experience.

Those who work for an idea are strong, powerful and dependable and Heaven relies on them. As for the others, they are here one day and gone the next and they will never really understand anything. Our Teaching is divine, and we must work for it so that the ideal of the Kingdom of God on earth and the notion of harmony and love may be disseminated throughout the world. In this way even your health problems will disappear. Yes, and this is why I say that the only true doctors, the only true healers on earth are Initiates, because they go to the roots of illness. Others intervene when it is already too late. Human beings should be cared for before they fall ill. As soon as disharmony (hatred, scandal-mongering, viciousness, envy and revolt) begins to gnaw at them, it is the beginning of illness. For an illness is a disorder and – what can you expect? – when one disorder meets another, they get along very well together! Whereas if harmony dwells within you, disorder cannot get in; your inner harmony stands in the way. It is important to know these laws.

You do so many things when in a state of disharmony: you embrace your wife or children or your friends when you are sad, worried or irritable. You often undertake even your most important tasks when you are in a state of disharmony: no wonder they are so rarely successful!

Every morning, when you first wake up, you should begin the day by attuning yourself to the world of universal harmony. Only then should you get your breakfast, talk to your children, kiss them and get them dressed, or go to work. When you go to visit someone, your first thought on entering their house should be: 'May peace and harmony reign in this house!' But don't delude yourselves: there are not many who think of doing this. They go in, and before you know it, they have sown discord between husband and wife or parents and children! And when you look at people in the street or shops, everywhere, even in schools, all one sees is their lack of harmony.

Many people imagine that their attitude of opposition and discord demonstrates that they are intelligent, responsible people. They pride themselves on disturbing the atmosphere; they think it is a sign of their power. If they only knew! It is so easy, the easiest thing in the world, to disrupt harmony. You only have to say something wounding, shoot a murderous glance at someone, make a threatening gesture or break something, and there you are! But it takes tremendous knowledge and a great deal of hard work to restore harmony!

The Laws of Harmony are the most solemn laws of the universe. Think about this, meditate and observe yourself and your reactions and see what state you are in when you act; then you will understand why, in certain cases, you fail to get good results. Even when your intention is good, if you yourself are not in harmony, the good you intended will not have the conditions it needs to manifest itself; in fact, you will be disturbing something in the invisible world. You must never undertake anything when you are in a state of disharmony, and this applies, above all, to the creation of children! Parents should be extremely vigilant on this point: if they do not unite in harmony to create a child, they will have cause to regret it for the rest of their lives, for Hell itself will enter into that child. People are willing to spend days and months preparing themselves and trying to obtain everything else in life, but one minute of their time is too much to spend on harmonizing themselves: they think that it is unimportant.

And yet harmony is the most effective weapon there is against illness. If you are ill it means that there is disorder within you; you have harboured certain negative thoughts, feelings or attitudes and they are reflected in your health. Why are they reflected in one organ rather than in another? Because all this is worked out with mathematical precision, depending upon which law you have broken. And now, if you want to get better, you must think of nothing but harmony: day and night you must strive to conform, to be synchronized, to accord and align yourself with Life, with limitless, cosmic Life. For this is what true harmony is. It is not enough to be in harmony with a few individuals: your husband or wife, your children, parents, neighbours and friends: you must be in harmony with Universal Life. Unfortunately, many people are in perfect accord with a few mediocre individuals and completely out of tune with Universal Life! Little by little, that lack of harmony filters into every nook and cranny of their being and takes possession of them and then, one day, it shows up in the form of illness.

Don't think that, in saying this, I exclude myself. Not at all, I tell myself all that I am telling you. If I am ill or have some aches and pains, I tell myself, 'You see? This shows that you still haven't attained the harmony that you are always talking about. Get to work!' I am just as much concerned by what I am talking about, as you are. You will probably say, 'In that case, you are not so tremendously advanced or highly evolved, either.' You are right, I am not so tremendously advanced! But the essential difference between myself and a great many others is that I understand the importance of harmony, whereas the others have still not understood. Certainly, there are still many things in me that need to be cleansed, purified, transformed, sublimated, vivified and resuscitated. I certainly don't claim to have been perfect when I came into the world! Even Initiates inherit flaws and failings. When they reincarnate they have to be born into families from which they inevitably inherit imperfections and illness. Yes, but then they work twice, three times, a hundred times harder than others to hasten the process of cleansing and purification. This explains how they manage to achieve a state of harmony much more rapidly than others. That's all. Don't imagine that when an Initiate is born, everything within him is absolutely pure, harmonious and divine! I know better: the reality is not like that at all! But that is not really the point: the point is that you must never excuse yourself on the grounds that you have inherited this or that failing from your parents. Instead, you should simply say, 'If I had deserved better, I would have been sent to reincarnate in a better family. It's not my parents' fault; it's my own. So now it is up to me to tidy everything up, and clean and purify myself.' And then, after a while, you will be rejuvenated, luminous and radiant. The only thing is, of course, that you have to be very strong-minded and very much aware; you have to take it seriously.

It is not difficult to know whether or not you have succeeded in achieving harmony: your whole being will tell you. When all your cells vibrate together in unison you cannot fail to feel it. If you drink a glass of water when you are thirsty, you don't need anyone to tell you when your thirst is quenched, do you? Similarly, when you attain a state of harmony, you don't need to be told: you feel the influx of tremendous forces, your aura pulses and vibrates, you are in a state of wonder and delight. And if, on the contrary, you are in a state of disorder and chaos, do you need to be told what a piteous state you are in? No, you know it already. In fact, if someone were to come and praise you when you were feeling like that, you would be so embarrassed you would want to disappear!

You see, the Invisible World wants to teach us by means of our own experience, and no one will be spared the lessons of experience! The trouble is that human beings do not understand this language, so they do not draw any conclusions from their experiences. And yet this is where your real work lies: in reflecting on your experiences and in drawing the right conclusions from them so as to go much further on the path of spirituality. But do you do this? No, you repeat the same sorry experiences all your lives long, and never do anything to improve things. You suffer, to be sure; you are not very proud of yourselves, to be sure; but you are so used to the prevalent disorder that you never react; you are content to survive. This won't do! Hurry up and understand that you must get out of that rut! And the best way to do so is to meditate on harmony, to wish for harmony, to long for harmony, to love harmony, to introduce it into everything you do, into every movement, every word, every look. Why does this seem so difficult?

Even in a Teaching like ours, capable though it is of bringing all human beings, all hearts and souls, together in this luminous understanding, there are many who are not really willing to understand. They prefer to open their minds and hearts to the prevailing currents of anarchy, rather than working for universal harmony. This is why I cannot be perfectly happy. Not that it really affects me, of course, for I have already attained this inner harmony. But my happiness is not yet complete because it necessarily includes your happiness and that of all men. As far as my own work goes, I have all that I need, I enjoy absolute happiness and fulfilment. But that is not the end of my task: my task is not that of many religious people whose one ambition was to save their own souls. My task is to do everything in my power to help others to achieve what I have achieved. But I am not succeeding. I try to lead them forward, to pull them after me, but they don't understand; they don't follow. This is why I cannot be completely happy: I have not been given the task of being happy all by myself, but of getting every human being to share this happiness.

If only you would take the trouble to understand these truths in greater depth, you would enjoy the same conceptions, the same light, the same plenitude that I enjoy, and then you would support and help me and, together, we could revolutionize the world and do good to every single human being. But I can sense that a great many of you cannot follow me; you don't want to understand. Your minds are full of all kinds of things that are in contradiction with what I tell you. This is what hurts and saddens me. I repeat: it is not for myself that I am saddened. I have already resolved a great many problems of my own. But my work is not to find happiness in doing the will of Heaven all alone but to carry you along with me!

From now on, therefore, instead of wasting your time thinking about all kinds of other things: your favourite amusements, your business deals, your love affairs, think about harmony; think about achieving harmony within your whole being, so that all your cells vibrate in unison. Take the example of an orchestra: you have all listened to orchestral concerts and know that it takes only one player playing out of tune to destroy the harmony of the whole orchestra. And that is exactly how it is with our physical bodies, our whole beings, for our organs are the instruments of an orchestra and they have to play together. Try to read when you have a splitting headache, diarrhoea or toothache: the disharmony within you prevents you from taking anything in, but once the pain has eased and things are back to normal you have no trouble understanding what you are reading.

There are quantities of examples in our every-day lives which can help us to understand the importance of harmony. An orchestra, a choir, a ballet, even a military parade: they all have to be harmonious. Everything in nature and in our own lives bears this lesson of harmony, order and beauty, but men continue to live in inner disorder and tumult! Ah, human beings... what a troublesome lot they are! They never agree to harmonize themselves with the laws of the universe. In fact, human beings are the only ones who are so recalcitrant: animals, insects and plants, the spirits of nature, the Angels... They are all in harmony except men! Yes, men are anarchists!

Henceforth, put everything else to one side and concentrate on the order established by God at the beginning of the world; in this way that primordial harmony will be restored within you. Every day, if only for a few minutes, project messages of love to all the luminous beings that people the universe. Tell them, 'I love you; I am attuned to you, I want to dwell eternally in your harmony.' Little by little, that harmony will soak into you and bring you light and joy, and you will feel so strong and resilient that you will not even be afraid of death any longer. Yes, thanks to harmony you will conquer death.

But, of course, there is one thing you have to remember, and that is that in order to attract harmony, in order to build it, you have to love it. As long as you don't truly love harmony and feel the need for it, you will never persuade it to come to you. But I can feel that you are beginning to love it and that you are making a sincere effort to create harmony in you and around you. Continue to do so and, one day, you will become aware of all the transformations taking place throughout the world because of the work we are doing here. Thanks to our existence here, we are helping to create a healthier climate in every corner of the world and inspiring a great many people who long to free themselves from the prevailing disorder. Yes, when we live in this harmony not only do we ourselves begin to taste the reality of the Kingdom of God but, above all, we are projecting into the world, and even as far as the stars in the heavens, currents, waves and forces of such power and splendour that, sooner or later, the whole of mankind will be obliged to improve and transform itself and to live in prosperity and peace.

Chapter Four

THE SPIRITUAL FOUNDATIONS
OF MEDICINE

There is no denying that modern medicine in the West, with its advances in surgical techniques, radiation treatment and so on, is very impressive. But why is it that more and more people, instead of getting better, are getting ill? Sometimes, I wonder if there are two really healthy people in the whole world! And the list of known diseases is getting longer and longer. Oh, I know: you will tell me that these diseases have always existed, but that we just did not know about them, so no attempt was made to cure them. There is some truth in that, but it is not entirely true. Nor do I agree with those who say that the new illnesses are entirely due to polluted air and water and adulterated foods. To be sure, factories release industrial wastes into the waterways, the air is fouled by smoke and toxic gasses, fruit and vegetables are cultivated with massive doses of chemical fertilizers, and the bread, butter, oil and everything else we eat, has been processed and tampered with! But all that is only the material aspect of the question, and the true causes of disease lie elsewhere: in the way human beings think and feel and behave. This aspect of the problem is never mentioned; no one ever explains that certain thoughts and feelings rot and ferment inside you and turn to poison. So everyone attempts to remedy their ailments by swallowing medicines, without realizing that it is by their thoughts and feelings that they destroy or restore their health.

In Europe, within the last twenty or thirty years, psychosomatic medicine has begun to recognize the role of the human psyche in illness and to explore the subtler aspects of man. But this subtle aspect is nothing new: it has always existed! Why do so many doctors still obstinately refuse to envisage anything but the material, physical aspects of illness? Forty or fifty years ago, they thought that the only thing that mattered was the number of calories the body needed to function properly; the discussion centred exclusively on the daily requirements of proteins, lipids, carbohydrates and mineral salts. Then came the discovery of vitamins, and the spotlight was switched from calories to vitamins, minute doses of which are far more potent than proteins and carbohydrates. And now, the latest discovery is the endocrine glands and the extremely subtle hormones they secrete, which are even more important than vitamins!

But for all their importance, the endocrine glands are not ultimately responsible for everything that goes on in our bodies: they only carry out orders received from elsewhere, and if, as sometimes happens, they secrete too much or too little, or cease to function altogether, it is because they are conditioned by other, much subtler factors, which medical research has not yet discovered. Yes, there are still many things to be discovered! It is the invisible dimension that controls the visible, the subtle world that takes priority over the physical, the spirit that is in command of matter. But our contemporaries still refuse to accept this. They believe that the subtle, psychic dimension depends on the material dimension, the physical body, and that thoughts, for example, are secreted by the brain just as bile is secreted by the liver whereas, in fact, it is the other way round, for thoughts are living beings. But I have already talked to you about this, so I shall not go into it again today.

Each human being possesses within himself the elements he needs to resist disease. Yes, there are cases of people who were considered terminally ill by their doctors and who managed to cure themselves. How? By will-power and thought. Of course, it is not everyone who can do this, you have to have developed certain faculties; but it is possible. I have already spoken to you, in another lecture, of plants whose roots do not need to be in the soil: they draw their vitality from the atmosphere. How can they do this? Well, if a plant is capable of getting all the elements it needs from the atmosphere in this way, how much more should man be capable of doing the same! Chemists will say, 'It's a question of chemical processes, it's purely chemical...' Yes, to be sure, everything is chemical, but chemistry is ruled by the spirit. The spirit is capable of producing curative chemical elements, but medical science still refuses to acknowledge the powers of the spirit, and this is where its great error lies.

In spite of this, I have to admit that medical science is beginning to be aware of the beneficial effects of harmony on human health: it recognizes that many illnesses are caused by a long standing condition of inner disharmony, disharmony in people's thoughts and feelings, etc. Doctors and psychologists have all kinds of scientific names for these illnesses, but I continue to refer to them in the simplest terms which are self-explanatory, and my name for all these illnesses is 'disharmony'. If you observe the effects of harmony and disharmony in every domain, in every activity and every area of society, whatever scientific label you choose to give them, it always boils down to a question of harmony or disharmony, order or disorder.

The progress of medicine over the centuries has been considerable; it has found cures for the plague, cholera, typhoid and tuberculosis, etc., but it has still not found ways of rescuing human beings from the disorders of the nervous system: anxiety, phobias, nervous collapse or depression which, in turn, have an extremely debilitating effect on the physical organism. And, as you know, illnesses move from one part of the body to another: in the past, certain parts were more affected and, nowadays, it is others: the nervous system or the heart, for instance. But there are new illnesses too, and some, such as poliomyelitis or cancer, are extremely difficult to cure.

I am very glad to see that the medical professions are beginning to change some of their positions, and that entirely new trends, closer to the truths of our Teaching, are becoming more and more apparent. As the explanations and points of view exposed in our Teaching are all part of the Initiatic Science that traces its origins to the earliest days of mankind, it shows that conventional medical science is gradually turning back to the great truths of the past. Recently, doctors have been somewhat disturbed by the widespread reactions against treatment with antibiotics and chemotherapy, which have sometimes had very negative effects. Some are beginning to turn to homoeopathy[1] because they

---

[1] This lecture was given in 1970.

realize that allopathic doctors treat the disease rather than the patient; they forget about the whole person with all his individual, specific characteristics. They have also seen that when they destroy the harmful microbes or viruses that cause illness, they often destroy useful micro-organisms at the same time.

Medical science is also beginning to realize that man's psychic faculties set him apart from all other categories of living beings. Doctors recognize that the same drug does not always have the same effect on different patients, which means that they cannot necessarily give the same remedies to all those who have the same illness. Good homoeopathic doctors study each individual patient in detail, taking into account his temperament, his psychic state and even his likes and dislikes, and then they prescribe a remedy that is suited to him, but which may be quite unsuited to someone else. They know that each patient must be seen within the framework of all the circumstances and elements which make up the 'terrain' or breeding ground of disease, whereas orthodox medicine, in concentrating on the illness itself, has neglected the conditions leading to its development.

There has also been a recent revival of interest in the principles taught by Hippocrates. Hippocrates was a Greek doctor who had studied the medical science of Egypt and India, and who taught that the most important thing was to help the body to defend itself against disease, for the organism – that is to say, nature – has its own system of defence. If a person's powers of resistance are developed to the full, they constitute such a formidable defence that the enemy is put to flight. You can see proof of this in the fact that, during an epidemic, some people care for the sick without being affected, whereas others, in spite of all their precautions, are carried off by the disease. Why? Because those who are immune offer a hostile terrain for the proliferation of microbes. Illness only attacks a man when it sees that his defences are weak.

Hippocrates used natural means to increase his patients' resistance to disease: baths, herbal infusions, sunbathing, rest, purification and fasting, etc. But, today, sick people take so many drugs that they actually weaken their natural system of defence; in relying so heavily on external means they fail to develop their own innate strength.

At the first suspicion of a minor upset, people rush to the medicine cupboard: is that a reasonable way to behave? Why not start by trying a natural remedy? If you have caught cold and are feeling shivery, for instance, get undressed and rub yourself energetically with a dry, rough towel or a loofah, then wrap yourself up warmly in blankets and drink several cups of hot water. This will make you sweat and help to make you better. Why not try my method? It is very simple and I have used it successfully dozens of times. Don't do what most people do: they wait until they are really ill and then it takes the whole arsenal of medical science to cure them! Don't put it off.

And don't take medicines indiscriminately either; if you are not careful about what you swallow your organism will soon be unable to defend itself against attack. A great many anomalies that we see today are the result of the abuse of pharmaceutical products. This is why, instead of pursuing more and more daring experiments in chemical and surgical techniques, research should take other directions. The physical environment of the sick, for instance, should be very different in order to awaken the powers dormant within them. Human beings have a built-in ability to manufacture antidotes for any harmful substance, but they lack the knowledge and they lack the will-power to put this ability to work; in other words, it is the spiritual dimension that is deficient.

Today, it is almost universally recognized that antibiotics and radiation therapy – ultraviolet, infra-red, cobalt rays, and so on – all have very harmful side effects. Yes, doctors are using new treatments experimentally before the side-effects that are liable to follow are fully known and, without their knowledge, many patients serve as guinea-pigs.

Or else they use animals; but what is good for animals is not necessarily good for human beings. Why should we suppose that a treatment that is successful on a mouse or a rabbit will necessarily succeed on a human being? Human beings are built quite differently from mice or rabbits! Besides, we do not have the right to kill thousands and thousands of animals for experimentation. It is a crime that humanity will have to pay for, one day.

If you read the Book of Genesis, you will see that it was only in the time of Noah that God allowed men to kill animals. Adam and Eve were allowed to eat only fruit and herbs. Later on, after they left the Ark, when men had already lost their innocence and light, the Lord allowed them to slaughter animals for food, while forbidding them to shed human blood, saying: 'Surely for your lifeblood I will demand a reckoning'! Well, for my part, I think that the blood of animals also demands a reckoning, and that many new illnesses come from this. Men will be required to shed as much of their own blood as they have shed of the blood of animals. It is only justice.

So, as I say, certain elements of the medical Establishment are turning back to Hippocrates and to nature. They are beginning to recognize the merits of sea water, for example; clinics of thalassotherapy are on the increase. Sea water contains all the substances that the body needs: exactly those elements that are to be found in our blood. The Egyptian doctors who cured Plato did so with thalassotherapy, and the ancient Babylonians, Chinese and Japanese also practised this type of therapy. It is a therapy with which I fully agree, for it corresponds to our Teaching which wants to teach man to regain his inner balance by drawing all the elements his body needs from the inexhaustible reservoirs of nature. The latest scientific discoveries confirm that man's body contains all the elements contained in the oceans, for, like all other living creatures, human beings came originally from the sea. When he is immersed once again in his primordial element, the sea, man is restored to his original equilibrium.

To drink sea water is also very good; it is a veritable transfusion, and one way of doing this is to eat oysters. Some people claim that the minerals found in sea water come from the rain and rivers and from ground-waters that have filtered through the soil, but the latest research shows that iodine, boron and other very rare elements found in the sea, are not found on dry land: it is still not known where they come from. You will ask, 'But can't you get the same substances from pills manufactured in a laboratory?' No, it is not the same thing; the elements you get from the sea are alive, and your organism absorbs and assimilates them more readily. I don't recommend the products that men manufacture in their factories and laboratories.

The ideal way would be to take baths of hot sea-water to which seaweed has been added for, as recent scientific research has shown, when the water is heated the elements it contains are absorbed into the blood stream, and seaweed also has remarkable therapeutic properties. As a matter of fact, my grandmother used to cure people this way, so I have known for more than sixty years that it is possible to restore the harmony of the body with hot baths of sea water and seaweed. It is also good to eat seaweed. The Japanese owe their remarkable powers of resistance to the fact that they eat a lot of seaweed. When I visited the Hawaiian Islands I saw shops that sold all kinds of fish and shellfish, and also several different kinds of seaweed; I have never seen or tasted anything of quite the same shape, consistency and flavour anywhere else. And people bought quantities of these seaweeds. How good it would be if we could get them here! They contain all the nutrients we need. Of course, you can buy them in specialized food shops, but you have to be careful about what you buy, for they are not always fresh, and you never know how they have been prepared. It would be so much better to go and collect them from the right places yourselves, but it is not easy, the seas are so polluted!

But how inconsistent people are! They recommend thalassotherapy and wax enthusiastic over the benefits of sea water and seaweed, but they never pause to wonder where the forces and energies transmitted by the sea come from. They always forget the one thing that matters: the sun! It is the sun that gives sea water and seaweed the vitality that human beings benefit from. It is the sun that is the vital factor: the water and plants are simply vehicles, transmitters. If the sea were not vivified by the sun it would have nothing beneficial to offer.

Human beings always miss the essential factor when they reason about something because they do not possess true knowledge: it never occurs to them that everything on earth comes from the sun. Take a tree, for example: what is a tree? Nothing more nor less than a storehouse of condensed sunlight. When you burn a tree, all that condensed light goes back to the sun, leaving behind it only a small quantity of gas, water vapour and earth in the form of ashes. And the oceans, like a tree, are simply reservoirs of sunlight. The sun looks down on the sea and fills it with its own life so that, when we bathe or drink its water, we, in turn, receive the life that comes from the sun.

I also recommend phytotherapy and aromatherapy, both of which use plants. Why? Because plants also have the property of receiving and condensing elements from the sun and stars. I have complete confidence in their therapeutic virtues and, if you know the right doses and how to combine them, they cannot do any harm. So I advise you to use plants as much as possible.

Yet another form of therapy that I recommend is the very ancient science of chiropractic, which was rediscovered by an American and has gradually spread to all the other countries. I have often emphasized the importance of the spine, and told you that many illnesses are caused by a deviation of the spinal column, a pinched nerve or an injured disc. Since the different organs are dependent on the nerves, it is no good trying to cure an organ if you do nothing about the nerves that supply it; and the nerves run through the spinal column. The spine is a bridge between the brain and the organs and the rest of the body, and if the bridge is in poor condition, it will inevitably lead to anomalies in the organs. The normal functioning of the organs must be restored, therefore, by taking care of the nerves that run through the spinal column. Those who are skilled in this science have cured many different illnesses including deafness which, in some cases, is due to a problem in the spine.

Magnetism is yet another form of therapy; in fact magnetism and phytotherapy are two of the most ancient therapeutic methods known to man. From the beginning of time Initiates have used magnetism to heal people. The Gospels tell us that Jesus touched the sick and healed them. How? By instilling into them a force, his own force, a harmonious, perfect fluid, as though he were injecting life into them. And what effect does life have? Exactly the same as that of the pure air you breathe into your lungs, or of a blood transfusion: it restores balance throughout the organism. When an Initiate touches someone who is ill, therefore, thanks to the fact that he himself lives a harmonious, fulfilled, divine life, he effects a veritable transfusion of vitality, a transfusion, as it were, of his own life-blood, and the sick person feels better. Yes, as I say, magnetism is the most ancient form of medicine; it is the medicine of the Initiates of old who healed with a touch, a glance or simply a word, without physical contact of any kind. It is, indeed, a kind of injection, for it consists in 'injecting' something into the sick person's body.

There are many more different kinds of therapy. Before the war, already, some were interested in cellulotherapy. They cured and prolonged life or retarded the ageing process by injecting into the human body a solution of cells taken from the glands, spleen, liver, kidneys, etc., of certain animals. This type of therapy has been known for centuries; in fact Paracelsus was familiar with it. It is known that there are still tribes in Africa and

America that eat certain animal organs in order to acquire the qualities of those animals. They believe, for instance, that by eating the heart of a lion they will acquire the strength and courage of a lion, whereas if they eat the heart of a rabbit they will become timid and fearful. And Serge Voronoff, for example, transplanted glands from monkeys into human beings in order to revive their flagging sexual activity, but the method was abandoned when it was found that although many people recovered their sexual energy, they also reverted to animality. In any case, to take cells from animals and graft them into human beings is certainly not something I recommend. It is true, therefore, that cellulotherapy can give good results, but it is a form of black magic, for it necessitates the sacrifice of living creatures. So this is one kind of therapy that I do not recommend; it is effective, to be sure, but you must find other methods.

Anything that is incompatible with the Science that I have studied, Initiatic Science, must be rejected. Initiatic Science takes the whole man into account, not just one part of his being or one organ: the liver, spleen or heart. A long time ago, Hippocrates said that a disorder in one part of the body always meant that the whole organism was perturbed. The first thing to do, therefore, is to restore harmony to the whole, and then the part

that is ill will be cured by the organism itself. In
any case, whatever remedies man may try, however
many pills, injections and antibiotics he takes, they
will always be ineffectual as long as his thoughts
and feelings continue to foster inner disorder.

Nor can I agree with methods that separate
beings or objects from the whole, from the universe,
in order to study and analyse them, for they only
succeed in killing the objects of their study. This is
no way to reach accurate conclusions! Analysis and
dissection are very ineffectual methods. As I have
often said, one must never cut things off from the
tree of life in order to study them. If you separate
something from its source you inevitably destroy
its beauty, light, radiance and vitality and reduce it
to the state of a cadaver. And this is what science
studies: cadavers. It has not yet learned to study
life. True, I sometimes analyse things myself, but
I do so in order to lead you towards the synthesis;
I never stop at analysis, for analysis destroys.

If you take a watch apart you will know exactly
how it was put together... the trouble is, though, that
it won't work any more! Biologists know exactly
what elements go to make up a man, but they are
incapable of putting all those elements together and
producing a human being, a living, thinking being,
capable of moving about and doing things. All the
elements may be there, but the essential factor, life,
is absent. And only life knows the exact quantities

and combinations and all the conditions necessary for a human organism to function smoothly. So we have to call on life to help us, for only life knows how to restore balance to the stomach, brain and lungs, to the whole body. But as biologists are not concerned with life but only with matter, they are unable to do this. As long as they do not rid themselves of their materialistic, mechanistic philosophy which separates the parts from the cosmic whole, they will never succeed in freeing mankind from disease. To be sure, their ideal is very noble, many of them make great sacrifices, they have extraordinary gifts of intelligence and skill, but their philosophy is false, and this is why so many things still escape them.

All the things I reveal to you are in harmony with this sublime philosophy that has been entrusted to me and which will be adopted, one day, by all men. Already science is finding itself obliged to turn, more and more, to the truths of the past. For example, chemists have long scoffed at alchemists who claimed to be able to transmute lead into gold and, then, not so very long ago, they discovered that an atom of lead had eighty-two electrons and an atom of gold seventy-nine, which means that if they could simply remove three electrons, three protons and a few neutrons from an atom of lead it would become an atom of gold! Unfortunately, it is not feasible to make any quantity of gold in

this way because it is unstable and, besides, the
process would be much too costly. But the beliefs
of orthodox science have recently suffered a few
shocks and such things as phrenology, telepathy
and divining are beginning to attract some
interest and, before long, astrology will also gain
recognition. One day everybody will be able to
see, hear and read about all these truths that I have
been revealing to you for years. More and more,
scientists will come to realize that the Ancients,
who had neither telescopes nor microscopes, made
many extremely important discoveries (who taught
them?), and when they come to study the teachings
of the Initiates seriously, all their theories will be
revolutionized. When this happens, the present
situation will be completely reversed: instead of
analysis and death, they will teach synthesis and
the science of life, and then the Kingdom of God
will become possible. But as long as the fortress
of orthodox materialistic science has not been
overthrown and replaced by the Science of the
Initiates, the present disorder will prevail.

Let me show you, now, why the medicine recommended by Initiatic Science is so much better than
all the others. As almost all doctors have studied
in universities which give priority to the physical
dimension, they neglect the way their patients live,
and their thoughts, feelings and general behaviour,

and yet it is these factors that should have priority. The only true therapy is the way one lives! All the other factors take second, third or fourth place!

Psychosomatic medicine studies the connection and interaction between a person's psychic state and his physical body. Psychosomatic medicine is gaining ground, and this is all to the good! But it will be far more effective when it is founded on a true philosophy, a true overall view of reality. And the starting point of this overall view is man, for man is the foundation on which everything else rests. No true progress can be achieved in any area whatever (scientific, economic, social, psychological or medical), as long as the structure of man, the forces that inhabit him and his relations with the universe are ignored or unknown, and it is this that Esoteric Science has been studying for thousands of years.

For a long time, scientists envisaged man as a kind of machine. Even now, in fact, many see him as a kind of clockwork motor; they make no provision for the idea that a human being is inhabited by forces, entities and intelligences still unknown to them, and that these living forces are capable of manufacturing new elements in his organism. They do not know that man possesses several subtle bodies; they have no idea of the true nature of thought or of the will and even less of the soul and the spirit or of the powers they possess. And yet, in spite of these shortcomings, they imagine that they are going to cure human beings of their illnesses! It is quite impossible! Yes, of course, the physical dimension is extremely important, but one also has to look at the higher dimensions, at the higher planes on which other forces and entities exist. What I am saying to you is based on authentic knowledge and, one day, mankind will be obliged to recognize this. A human being is much more than the visible, tangible being before us, but he does not know himself... and medical science does not know him either! Yes, medical science is still treating beings that it does not understand: how can it hope for good results?

The first thing to realize is that, above and beyond his physical body, man has other, subtler bodies: the etheric body which impregnates the physical body and which is the vehicle of vitality and memory; the astral body, the body of feelings and emotions, and the mental body. I have often talked to you about these different bodies, etheric, astral, mental, Causal, Buddhic and Atmic,[2] so I shall not discuss them today. But take the case of someone whose etheric body is not properly attached to his physical body: he will feel that something is wrong, but the doctors will be unable

---

[2] See *Man's Psychic Life: Elements and Structures,* Izvor 222, chap. 3: 'Several Souls and Several Bodies'.

to find the cause of his discomfort, for his physical body is perfectly normal. So far, doctors are incapable of treating the etheric body, and as long as they refuse to recognize the existence of man's subtle bodies, it is no use their hoping to achieve the complete cure of disease!

Yes, the first thing to do is to study man, for man is the key to the universe. As long as you do not possess that key, you will find yourself faced with insoluble problems. It is time that researchers gave man first place; when they do so they will discover his invisible dimensions: his aura, his emanations and vibrations, his symbiotic relationship with the entities of nature and the different worlds, his ability to travel through space, to tune in to waves, to see and act at a distance, etc. And then everything will be changed. When you are concerned with man, you are at the very heart of things, for man is truly the key to all mysteries.

And now, which therapeutic methods should be given first place? Those that I have mentioned so far: chemotherapy, phytotherapy, thalassotherapy, chiropractic, are not the most important. The best and most effective therapy is to think, feel and act in harmony with the luminous forces and beings of nature and the whole universe. This means that men must know these forces and entities and attune themselves to them. This is the sovereign form of medicine. I do not reject the other forms, of course, and it is not when somebody is gravely ill that one should start preaching to him about changing his eating habits and his way of life! It is often necessary to intervene very rapidly and give antibiotics or a blood transfusion or even operate. But it is still important to understand that the best form of medicine is that which is practised every day by the way one lives, that is to say, the way one thinks, feels, believes, loves and nourishes oneself.

This is why it is so important that doctors, instead of focusing only on disease, should start focusing their attention on health and the factors conducive to good health (respiration, nutrition, behaviour); it is very important, also, that the laws of good health should be taught to all. If this were done it would no longer be necessary to spend millions on more and more expensive research laboratories and hospitals.

Unfortunately, if you listen to the doctors who are interviewed on television or on the radio, you will never hear them mention the way people live: they only talk about new treatments, vaccines, radiation therapy, operations and so on, so that those who listen to them get the impression that they can continue to live as they please and commit every sort of excess, without regard for laws or rules of any kind. What does it matter? The doctors

will find ways of curing them and allowing them to
go on living their untidy lives! Yes, and this is why
governments will be obliged to go on spending
billions on health care until people discover, at last,
that what matters most is very simple: it is the way
one lives.

To be sure, one cannot help but admire some of
these doctors: their discoveries and the sacrifices
they make are extraordinary! And yet, one is
obliged to admit that much of their effort has been
wasted because they have not known in what
direction to look.

Some of you may want to object that if good or
bad health depends on one's way of life, children
should never be ill, because they have not had time
to have evil thoughts and feelings or to do anything
wrong. At first sight, this seems to be true, but only
if you do not know that we all live on this earth
more than once. When a child is ill it is because
of the way he lived in previous incarnations: if he
has been born into a family from which he inherits
certain defects or weaknesses, it is because this is
what he has deserved. So the rule is always valid:
the most important factor is the way we live, the
way we think and feel and act. If you have still
not understood this, not only will you be unable to
remedy the problems of your present lives, but you
will be preparing very unfavourable conditions for
your future incarnations. Accept the truths taught

by the great Initiates for, as long as one has not studied Initiatic Science, one is bound to draw erroneous conclusions. Tell yourselves, 'Since there are so many things that I don't understand, I'd better make up my mind to trust this divine Science and give priority to the way I live.' After that, you can add all the other forms of therapy you like: but the way you live comes first!

There is yet another form of therapy which I referred to indirectly a few moments ago, and that is the therapy of the sun. One day, the whole of mankind will turn to the sun, which is an inexhaustible reservoir; it is the sun that will effect the most complete cures but, here again, only if we live as we should: the way we live will always be the foremost therapy. When man lives according to the laws of God, he will not need clinics and hospitals any longer. At the moment, the only solution seems to be to build more and more hospitals, because there are more and more sick people and more and more varieties of disease. Yes, because the way men live and think is becoming worse and worse. They are becoming more and more knowledgeable and learned, but their health is getting progressively worse. It is very worrying for, on the one hand, there is evolution and, on the other, there is what can only be called degeneration. And it is no good thinking that the situation can be remedied by material elements, for God has not given the gift of absolute efficacy to matter: matter can never provide more than a temporary relief.

Human beings give their physical bodies the food and drink they need, but man is more than a physical body: he is also a soul and a spirit, and the soul and spirit cannot be fed on meat and potatoes... or hormones! And as science makes no provision for the needs of men's souls and spirits, they are left to suffer from hunger and thirst. This is why we see so many people who seem to have everything they could possibly need: a good job, a family, a house and car, etc., and yet, deep down, they feel an emptiness, they are dissatisfied. This is a sure sign that they have forgotten their soul; as for their spirit, it just doesn't come into it! The medicine of the future will be obliged to take into account all the needs of human beings, including those of the soul and spirit, and to supply them with the elements lacking to them.

Understand what I am saying: our Teaching will give you neither houses nor cars nor fine clothes, but you will find in it all that you need to satisfy your soul and spirit. And when the soul and spirit are satisfied, they have a beneficial effect on the physical body and new processes are set in motion. And then, even if your physical body is not very well dressed or has not had much to eat, it can hold up its head with self-respect. Yes, our Teaching gives you the most precious and indispensable elements you need for your equilibrium and happiness.

We all know that many patients would be cured if their doctor would only give them just a few kind words, but as he is always in a hurry, he writes a prescription and rushes off to his next appointment. Many doctors think that love, hope and encouragement are not important; in fact, they often actually kill their patients by telling them that they cannot be cured and have only a few months or days to live. Fortunately, some doctors do realize that they must have a friendly relationship with their patients; they know that medicines are not the only things that can cure people. In the past, many doctors were true apostles, but nowadays, as often as not, they are mere mercenaries. In fact, in the United States, there are patients who never even see a doctor: their illness is diagnosed by electronic instruments and, depending on the results, they may see the doctor or, equally, they may not, in which case they will receive their prescription by post! Yes, there is no more human contact; everything is automated and love goes by the board. And yet, the only thing that heals is love!

One day all this will change and men will discover that it is love, trust and hope that is so sorely missing, that the cause of all their ill health is doubt, distrust and disharmony. This is why I repeat and insist that the most potent of all therapies is the way you live. To be sure, I cannot promise you that its curative effects will be as rapid as those of a drug. When you take a pill you feel the effects almost at once. But do they last? And can you continue to take pills without suffering from side effects? The kind of medicine I recommend acts slowly, but it is safer and, in the long run, it is the most effective. The only thing is that it presupposes a truthful, authentic, all-embracing philosophy of life, because it is what we think that determines everything else.

And when I speak of philosophy, I am referring to the one and only philosophy which was not elaborated by the human intellect but was discovered by the great Initiates, thanks to their exceptional gifts of clairvoyance and astral projection. And I can tell you this: Heaven has chosen me to be an heir to this divine philosophy. Without it, it is impossible to find the true path; we shall always lose our way. This is why I give absolute priority to this philosophy which teaches us how to live in harmony with all the different forces and worlds that exist, so that we need no longer be torn apart by inner conflict and contradiction. It reveals, also, the intimate structure of man and the exchanges his soul and spirit need to make with the forces of nature. Just as inevitably as a man's physical body dies if he is deprived of that indispensable form of exchange provided by respiration so, too, a man will die if his soul and spirit are not allowed to breathe, that is to say, if they are never given the opportunity to give and receive from the cosmos.

Remember, therefore, to keep your links with the forces of nature intact: if you do this you will be given the light to see the universe as a structure, as the most marvellous edifice imaginable, in which everything is connected, from the summit to the base; and when you see this clearly, you will be capable of restoring order and remedying many of the anomalies within you. Why don't you appreciate the value of all the truths I have given you? Because I am not famous or well known? As far as I am concerned, fame is not important: the only thing that matters is to discover truth. I have given my whole life to this and I cannot say that I am particularly interested in all the rest: fame and recognition. Besides, recognition will come without my having to look for it, for when you possess the truth, sooner or later, you receive recognition. And if you are in error, that, too, will always be recognized in the end: even if everyone applauds you now, one day you will simply be forgotten. No, no; I am working for something that can never be either replaced or forgotten.

What matters most, therefore, is to learn how to live, how to think, feel and act. On other occasions, in explaining the process by which plants and fishes, and even babies in their mother's womb, were formed, I spoke of the law of affinity, and showed you how man's thoughts and feelings forged links with kindred entities, forces and elements in space, and how, ultimately, these entities and forces came and attached themselves to him. Yes, it is an absolute law that man attracts to himself whatever he has formed ties with, and in this law can be found the explanation for all health or sickness, strength or weakness, intelligence or stupidity, beauty or ugliness, and so on. They are simply elements that we have attracted to ourselves.[3]

This means that if you are experiencing difficulties in your present life it is because of your ignorance in the past which caused you to perturb the right order of things. But now, thanks to this Initiatic philosophy which teaches you how to go about improving your thoughts and desires, you are in a position to form ties with the most highly spiritual entities and regions, and build a new body that will manifest all the qualities you want: health, strength and beauty. This is the secret of resurrection. If you are willing to understand and apply this science of life, you will have the power not only to defend yourselves against disease, but

---

[3] See *Man, Master of His Destiny,* Izvor 202, chap. 5:'The Laws of Correspondences'.

also to rebuild your body as you would like it to be. To be sure, for the time being, it may resist your efforts, but that is because you have been working unconsciously for hundreds of years to disfigure it, so it is going to take a long time to restore it to perfect health. But what I tell you is absolute. Six or seven years are sufficient to get a degree in medicine, but the Science of life is so vast that it takes thousands of years to possess it!

When men finally understand what their soul and spirit need, they will also understand that they have to be stirred to activity and put to work. Everything else depends on this work of the soul and spirit: they are the cause and all the rest is consequence. When you know that you are working on the level of causes (the level at which forces are set in motion), you can live in peace and security, for you also know the effects which are bound to follow. And this is how we can begin to cure psychic illness: by giving men knowledge and certainty. It is because man does not consciously relate to the luminous forces of nature by means of his soul and spirit that he is disorientated and tormented and has this sense of emptiness. But once light dawns in him, it reveals his links with Immensity and Eternity, and he realizes that he is capable of communicating with the forces of the cosmos and of transforming his life. And then, certainty and joy are his constant companions. If you do not enlighten people it is almost useless to try to heal them. They need this light, and they need it from earliest childhood. You can only help human beings to solve their physical and psychic problems by teaching them the truth about their own nature, and by showing them how they are linked to the Tree of Life and how they can draw from it the strength they need to work and transform themselves.

Never forget this: what matters most is this philosophy and the way you live; but, on the physical plane, it is the sun that must have priority. One day, science will study the question of how the sun can cure one: at what time of day and for how long one should sunbathe; how to put water into transparent coloured containers and expose it to the light of the sun, and when to drink it; how to use certain instruments to extract the curative elements from sunlight and how to work with sunlight in all its forms. How wonderful it will be when that day comes! At the moment, science attaches little importance to the sun because it is only interested in matter, in chemical elements. And yet, if sea water, seaweed, herbs and trees, and even gems and crystals, can cure, it is because they have received their curative powers from the sun. The sun will be the last to be appreciated, but once man discovers it, he will be obliged to give it priority: men will eat and drink the sun, breathe the sun, and even listen to the music of the sun, for they will have instruments capable of tuning in to it. Yes, the most beautiful music is that which comes from the sun. The most excellent messages, also, and, one day, men will be able to listen to broadcasts from the sun. Are you wondering whether I am talking seriously? Yes, I am not joking: I am speaking absolutely seriously.

The therapy of the future will be the therapy of the sun, and we shall apply it by watching the sunrise, by forming a bond of affection with the sun, by concentrating strongly on it in order to receive its particles. Science still knows nothing about the etheric particles that abound in every ray of sunlight. And yet, although modern medical science has still not acknowledged the existence of the more subtle aspects of matter, it has already realized that it is the imponderable elements in the body that are the most important for health. After attempting to cure the ailments of the digestive, circulatory, respiratory and excretory systems of their patients, in other words, after attempting to treat the sick organs, scientists finally discovered the endocrine glands whose imperceptible secretions block or stimulate the activity of the organs.

But the endocrine glands are not the be-all and end-all of scientific discovery: they, in turn, depend on other, subtler centres and, ultimately, on thought. It is as though the thought processes themselves contained glands which controlled the whole physical organism. One day, science will discover that there is a hierarchical structure that embraces every level of human existence, from thought to the physical organs. Yes, I don't believe that the endocrine glands are the most important, for they themselves depend on other factors. Man injures or improves his physical health by means of his thoughts and feelings which, in turn, influence his glandular system. Even growth or the cessation of growth, increase or loss of weight, etc., cannot be attributed only to the action of the endocrine glands.

It is interesting to note that science is working with progressively subtler elements. Still in the field of medicine, we find that homoeopathy uses remedies potentized to the 31st centesimal. Anyone would think that there could be no curative power left in them, and yet they are highly effective. And physicists, too, are discovering aspects of matter that are more and more subtle: after protons and neutrons, they have now found what they call mesons and neutrinos. When they finally reach the etheric dimension of matter, they will find particles and energies which are still unknown today, and which originate in the sun. A whole new science will grow up around the study of the sun's rays. In fact, instead of buying our vitamins from the chemist we shall go and get them from the sun. The vitamins that we buy at the pharmacy cannot be properly assimilated by our bodies; it is far better to get them from the fruit and vegetables in which the sun has stored them. The properties of even the most commonplace vegetables such as onions, leeks and radishes are still largely unknown. In fact, you should also eat the leaves of radishes: they are very tasty and contain more nutrients than the radishes themselves... and turnips, also, are very good for you!

In concluding I want to tell you, again, that if you know how to breathe, eat and drink, you will get your vitamins from all those elements in which the sun has put them, for the most important factor of all is the psychological attitude with which you receive things. You can swallow vitamin pills from morning to night, but if you have the wrong attitude, they will not make you any stronger. In fact, they would probably cause other problems in your digestive or circulatory system. Doctors never talk about the importance of one's state of consciousness or of the inner attitude we should have towards things: this is why the medicines they prescribe are even less effective than they might be. So, here again, we have a vitally important factor: our inner attitude towards what we receive.

Many people tell me, 'Master, when I am with you, I think and feel and act differently; problems seem to disappear; everything goes swimmingly! But as soon as I have been away from you for any length of time, nothing is the same: I find myself back in the workaday reality of life; I seem to be less convinced about the Teaching, and all that you have told us seems to fade away.' And my reply is that I experienced exactly the same thing, when I was young, in relation to my own Master, Peter Deunov. But if I am with you, now, it is in order to help you not only to accept a certain number of truths, but also to make an effort to keep them alive within you for as long as possible. Life is terribly hard, you say? Don't I know it! We constantly have to struggle, to face up to difficulties of all kinds, and we get tired! Yes, I know: life is difficult. I am not going to explain, now, why it is like that, but I am here, with you, precisely to help you to understand that if you accept the light of this Teaching, you will have much more strength and courage, and you will always know peace and hope.

When you go home, therefore, make an effort to keep the truths that you have received here vibrant and alive within you. Don't forget them. Tell yourself: 'I know that I can't escape from the realities of everyday life, but I must cling to these truths so as to be forewarned and forearmed for when hesitation, discouragement and negative thoughts come along. Whatever happens I will not give in; I refuse to be dragged down; I refuse to let

go of my enthusiasm and hope! I will not let my
flame be snuffed out.' Yes, cling to the truths I give
you, take a few deep breaths of oxygen and then
take the plunge and go and face reality! In this way
you will be strong and very powerful, and become
a source of life. Isn't that a much better prospect?

So many of you say, 'Ah, now I understand!
From now on I'll be stronger. You'll see!' And
then, when difficulties arise, they give up the
struggle once again. When they come back here,
of course, they are ashamed of their weakness, and
resolve to do better in future: 'You'll just see; I'll
not give in.' No, not until next time! So, the wisest
solution is to keep coming back until you really do
become staunch and unwavering. This is what the
Teaching is all about: becoming unwavering and,
whatever the circumstances, remembering that you
are immortal and that God has given you all the
powers you need. If you forget this, it will be the
end of you!

Understand what I am saying! Oh yes, I can
see that you are thinking, 'But I do, I do!' No, I'm
afraid you don't! You have not yet reached the
kind of understanding that I am talking about. To
understand me means to be as firm as a rock in
your convictions. Some of you have this firmness,
but not all. As soon as they find themselves back
in the turmoil of life, they allow themselves to be
influenced by the materialistic mentality that is

only interested in success and physical well-being and never spares a thought for the needs of the soul and spirit.

Believe me, you must discard this materialistic philosophy, for it will weaken you and make animals of you. If you want proof of this, you only have to see what happens to someone who is convinced that he is made only of matter, that the soul does not exist, that there is no life after death: he is capable of every ignoble act, and no wonder! How can you expect anything else? But the real tragedy is that when you put all these ideas into his head you destroy his will to do something sublime, you destroy the power of the spirit; in other words, you kill him! Whereas if you can get him to realize that he possesses a spirit and that, if he gave his spirit the opportunity to manifest itself he would be capable of greatness, you would be putting real power into his hands: his body would begin to obey him and respect his orders; he would no longer be bowled over by privations, misfortunes or illness; he would grow every day in strength and power and become a leader for others! But if he adopts the philosophy of materialism, he will be nothing. This is the danger of giving priority to the physical body, to matter, to the external, objective dimension. To be sure, the full extent of the damage caused by that attitude does not show up at once, but little by little, the human being sickens and dies. Reread my lecture about the strength of the spirit;[4] it will give you all the elements you need in order to advance and overcome your difficulties. Yes, the philosophy you must adopt, henceforth, is that of the spirit. Don't listen to those weak, stupid people who want to drag you down into the dust. It is true, we are matter, we are made of dust, but only part of us: the other part is divine.

The only thing that interests me is this philosophy that I patiently continue to transmit to you, and which contains all the possibilities you need to evolve to an infinite degree. Any philosophy, in fact, that fails to recognize that man has an infinite capacity for growth is incapable of teaching him the true meaning of life and you must not follow it.

---

[4] See *Life Force* C.W. 5 , chap. 8: 'The Strength of the Spirit'.

Chapter Five

RESPIRATION AND NUTRITION

For every human being, life on earth begins with a breath. Thanks to his first inhalation, a child's lungs fill with air and begin to do their work: life is set in motion. And many years later, when we are told that he has 'breathed his last', we understand that he has died. Yes, breath is the beginning and the end: life begins with an inhalation and ends with an exhalation.

It is worth taking the time to reflect on the function of respiration, to understand that it is at the root of life and also to practise it so that it may do its work more and more efficiently. In most human beings, this function is handicapped or, in some way, diminished or contaminated. This is why they need to learn to work with air so as to revive, purify and intensify the life within them.

One way of reaching a better understanding of the phenomenon of breathing and of the laws that govern it is to compare it with the process of nutrition.

What do you do when you eat? Before sending the food down to the stomach to be digested, you chew it. The mouth is like a little kitchen in which the food is prepared, cut up, cooked and seasoned with a little oil (that is, with saliva) by glands especially prepared for the purpose. This is why it is recommended to chew your food for a long time, until it is almost liquid. If you swallow it without chewing it sufficiently beforehand, it is not really ready to be digested and your organism cannot assimilate it completely; the result is an excessive amount of waste. Also, if your food is insufficiently chewed before it reaches your stomach, the body has to expend much more energy to assimilate it; you need look no further to find the cause of much of your fatigue.

You must not think that fatigue is always the result of overwork. No, it is very often caused by a waste of energy, and you are wasting energy when you swallow your food without chewing it properly and without having impregnated it with your thoughts and feelings, for it is more indigestible and much more difficult to assimilate.

You must realize that, in order to undertake spiritual work of any kind, you have to protect your organism and be careful not to demand wasteful expenditures of energy from it. Some people think that, in order to be healthy, active and invulnerable they have to eat a lot. No, that is not so. In fact, I suggest that you try the following experiment one day: chew every mouthful of food for as long as you can, for several minutes if possible, until it disappears completely in your mouth. You will find that, although you have eaten very little, you will have absorbed enough energy to last you several hours. If I mention this experiment, it is because I often practised it when I was young, in Bulgaria. As a student I was very poor and often had very little to eat, and I discovered that if I chewed my food for a long time I felt better nourished than when I ate at a normal speed. This showed me that food contained energies that we have not yet learned to liberate and use.

And, still on this subject, let me add that you should not leave the table feeling completely satisfied; it is better to have a slight sensation of hunger. Why? So as to leave some work for your etheric body to do. If you still have this slight feeling of emptiness, your etheric body is motivated to look for other, subtler nourishment on a higher level and, in a few moments, not only will you no longer feel hungry, but you will feel full of new energy, both physical and psychic. Whereas, if you eat your fill, you inhibit the activity of your etheric body and this is very bad for your health, for it means that your whole organism is in danger of stagnating.

You must not paralyse your etheric body but always stimulate it to be active, to have something to do, something to look for. It is thanks to this activity of your etheric body that you will be in good health. And, if you want to encourage the etheric body to become active, you must take care not to gorge your physical body; on the contrary, a very slight sensation of deprivation felt by the physical body prompts the etheric body to work harder.

But let's get back to the analogies between nutrition and respiration.

The two processes are governed by the same laws. Just as it is bad to swallow your food without chewing it, it is bad, also, to breathe so rapidly that the air does not have time to expand your lungs and fill them right down to the bottom. You must draw deep, slow breaths and even, from time to time, hold the air in your lungs for a few seconds before breathing out again. Why? In order to 'chew' it. Yes, your lungs are capable of 'chewing' air, just as your mouth chews food.

When we chew our food, the mouth does the work of a stomach with the subtler elements of the food. This question has not been given enough attention. The mouth is a subtle, spiritual stomach and its work is more important than that of the stomach, for the stomach receives only the coarsest parts of your food from which the subtle, etheric elements have been extracted by the mouth. You can verify this for yourself: take the case of someone who has been ill and has had no food for several days; he will, naturally, feel very weak, but give him some fruit, for instance, and hardly will he have begun to chew it (before he has had a chance to swallow it) than he will begin to feel his strength coming back. This proves that there are cells, glands, in the mouth and that they are the first to enter into action and to extract from your food the elements which are the most alive and the richest in energy. When their work is done, the coarser elements are sent on to be dealt with by the stomach.

People who eat too much and gulp down their food greedily send quantities of unchewed matter into their stomachs before their mouths have had a chance to extract the subtle elements. Perhaps they will build up strong bones and muscles in this way, or have a little more blood in their veins, but their nervous system will not be nourished. The health of the nervous system depends on the work that is done in the mouth. If you want to have inexhaustible reserves of nervous energy and be in command of your physical body and your emotions and feelings, chew your food for a long time, slowly, consciously and with love. Try it! You will see that your nervous system will be

considerably strengthened. Most people eat too
fast and swallow their food without chewing it
and then, for the rest of the day, they are nervous
and irritable. Self-education must begin with a
conscious, sensible way of eating. He who respects
the laws of nutrition will feel calm and unruffled,
he will achieve control, self-mastery and peace.
Do you want to be in control of your nerves? Then
begin by learning to eat correctly!

Now we can understand by analogy, how the
laws of nutrition are also the laws of respiration.
When you take a breath of air it is like taking a
mouthful of food, a mouthful of extraordinary
forces. If you let it out again too quickly, the lungs
don't have time to 'cook', 'digest' and assimilate
it sufficiently for the body to benefit from what it
contains. This is why so many people are tense,
tired and irritable: they don't know how to nourish
themselves with the air they breathe; they don't
'chew' it; they let it out immediately. Also, most
people breathe only with the upper part of their
lungs and the result is that the stale air is never
driven out and replaced by pure air. Deep breathing
is a magnificent exercise which you should practise
regularly, for it renews one's energies.

You all know how the engine of a car or a
motor cycle works: you feed it with petrol, which
is simply food in liquid form. When the spark
ignites the petrol vapour it transforms it into gas

(the element air), and this transformation produces the energy which makes a motor vehicle move. Well, the same thing happens when we eat: at each successive phase of disintegration in the mouth, stomach and so on, the food releases a certain amount of energy.

Our food is thus made to pass through progressively subtler states in our bodies. When we chew it, it becomes liquid and releases a certain form of power, for the gaseous element, escaping from the liquid which compressed and imprisoned it, needs to spread and expand and, in doing so, it triggers other processes. Subsequently, the gaseous element releases an etheric element, giving rise to even greater power which goes to nourish other regions and set other elements in motion. This is the secret of life.

Why do we eat? In order to release the energy that is locked up in food. And where does that energy come from? From the sun. Yes, it is the sun that has compressed its energy into the fruits and vegetables that we eat. It sends it to earth and the plants and vegetables absorb it in an etheric form and then condense it so that it takes up very little space. And animals and men, when they eat, do exactly the reverse, for to eat is to disintegrate matter in order to release the forces stored up in it by the sun.

Yes, the sun injects its energy into the whole of nature. Even rocks are full of it. This is why it is a good practice, if you are up in the mountains or in the country in warm, sunny weather, to find a large, flat rock that has been warmed by the sun, and to stretch out on it; it has a very powerful healing effect.

The sun pours tremendous quantities of energy into nature for the benefit of the creatures that absorb it, and this energy is present in the air in a form that Hindus call prâna. The best time of day in which to absorb the subtlest and most powerful element from the prâna is in the few minutes just before the sun rises. This is when it is present in greatest abundance. So, go and watch the sun rising: it is so soft and gentle... one feels almost as though one could drink it and it is only with the greatest effort that one can tear oneself away: it hurts to have to leave it and go back to one's everyday activities!

What matters most, then, is not to absorb the greatest possible quantity of food or liquid or air, but to assimilate them properly. And, in order to do this, one has to hold on to them long enough to extract all the virtue from them. Do you know how much energy is contained in a mouthful of bread? Try to guess... Well, I'll tell you: enough to pull a train with a hundred wagons round the world three times! And if this is so, why is it that our 'train' can only go a few yards on a mouthful? Because we have not managed to extract all the energy it contains.

And the same applies to the air you breathe: if you want to get the greatest possible benefit from it, you have to compress it and hold it in your lungs. While your lungs are holding the air under compression, your organism is doing a work which is the equivalent of the phases of ignition and explosion in an internal combustion engine and, as the air is prevented from escaping, it is forced to circulate through the tiny channels that nature opens for it. If you expel it at once and let it escape, all its energy is lost. When you hold it in, on the other hand, nature steers the energy it contains along these minute paths in your organism in such a way that it touches and sets in motion various centres as it passes.

Similarly, when you attend the sunrise in the morning, if you don't capture and hold on to the sun's rays, if you let them slip past you and don't use them, they will do nothing, they will be completely ineffective. But if you catch and hold on to them consciously, if you collect and compress them inside you, you will be opening a path for them into your spirit. Then they will move through you with tremendous force, setting in motion powerful centres, and you will feel yourself becoming a whirlwind of fire.

Even what you drink should be held in your mouth for a few moments. When I first became a disciple of the Master Peter Deunov, my liver was not working too well so, one day, I asked the Master

what I should do to cure it. This is what he said,
'Take several sips of hot water and keep it in your
mouth, take the time to taste it and swallow it only
very slowly and gently, while you think of the water.
Do this several times a day and you will be cured.'
'What a peculiar idea!' I thought; 'How can I possibly
be cured by drinking a few mouthfuls of water and
thinking about it?' I could not believe it; it was too
simple. But the Master gave me no other explanation
and it was only later that I understood. Of course,
if your liver is seriously affected you cannot cure it
simply by drinking hot water, but do this exercise
from time to time, it can only be beneficial.

The great secret, you see, is to transform each
element into one of greater subtlety: to liquefy
what is solid, to transform liquids into gases, to
transform gaseous elements into ether. He who
is capable of doing this possesses the secret of
how to draw constantly from the inexhaustible
Source. All living beings do this to a certain extent,
unconsciously – this is what makes it possible
for them to remain alive – but they don't do it
fully; they do it mechanically, without thinking
about what they are doing, and when it is done
unconsciously, the results are not the same as when
it is done consciously. To make matter subtler is
to release the energy it contains. All that is dense,
compact and heavy represents unorganized matter
in which energy is held prisoner. And the more

energy one imprisons within oneself (like those who overeat), the more harm one does to oneself. We must, on the contrary, liberate energy, and this is the function of breathing during meals: it allows a greater quantity of energy to be released from the food. As I have often said, nutrition is a form of combustion, and fire is constantly in need of air to revive it; that is why we blow on it. If you take a few deep breaths while you are eating, the combustion of your food will be more complete. It is enough to pause three or four times in the course of a meal and breathe deeply: in this way, greater energy will be released from your food.

Our role is not to condense or materialize energy; it is already sufficiently condensed. Our role is, rather, to set it free, to release it. The great Initiates, who know this law of the disintegration of matter, are capable of disintegrating a few thousandths of a milligram of the matter of their brain and, with the resulting energy, of working miracles. They effect this disintegration by means of thought; it is a secret that has been in their possession for thousands of years. They apply the principles of nuclear fission to their own brain which consists of a type of matter that contains inexhaustible wealth.

Perhaps some of you will say, 'Well, I'm capable of disintegrating matter, too. The other day I had a temperature of more than forty degrees, and I lost ten pounds!' That is not the same thing:

a true release of energy must make you stronger, not weaker! A fever debilitates you and leaves you weaker because it destroys a great many cells: you lose matter without gaining energy. Whereas someone who concentrates or meditates disintegrates some minute particles of matter and, in doing so, releases energy. And this is all the more beneficial and salutary in that other, purer, more luminous particles come to take the place of those that have been destroyed. This is not the case when you are ill or when there is a loss of energy from some other cause. You must distinguish an expenditure of energy that enriches you from one that impoverishes you.

As I have said, in order to release the etheric elements contained in air, you have to 'chew' it. The lungs are composed of several different zones, one of which can be compared to the mouth and another to the stomach, although their position in relation to each other is reversed. As a matter of fact, if you look at a pair of lungs you can see that they look like a tree with a trunk, branches and leaves. But it is standing on its head; the leaves of a tree are at the top, whereas the 'leaves' of the lungs (the alveoli) are at the bottom. A tree relates to the external gaseous atmosphere through its leaves, whereas air penetrates into the lungs through the 'trunk and branches'.

And now, if you take the comparison with the digestive system one step further, you will see that the lower part of the lungs has the same function as a mouth, whereas the upper part functions like a stomach. When we eat, we put food into the upper part of the digestive tract, the mouth, where it is chewed before being sent down to the stomach. When we breathe deeply, we do just the opposite: the air goes all the way down to the bottom of the lungs, to the alveoli which have the function of 'chewing' it, as though they were a mouth. Otherwise, if our breathing is shallow, the air remains in the upper part (the 'stomach') of the lungs without being chewed. You must practise breathing deeply, from the abdomen; if you don't send the air down to the bottom of your lungs, you can only extract the coarsest, least subtle particles from it. But if you send it all the way down, so far down that it pushes against the diaphragm, and keep it there for a few seconds, the 'mouth' of the lungs has a chance to function and to draw the subtler elements from the air and distribute them throughout the body.

But to obtain these subtle elements from the air, you must not only hold it in your lungs, you must also bring it up very slowly to the upper lobes so that it exerts pressure on them, for the function of the upper lobes is quite different from that of the lower lobes. Science will discover all these things in the future; every cell of an organism, even the different cells within the same organ, are differentiated and specialized and have their own place according to their own particular function in that organ. The way in which the cells in the lower part of the lungs absorb air is different from the way of those in the upper parts. It is just as bad for your health to breathe superficially, therefore, as it is to swallow your food without chewing it. By breathing deeply you nourish yourself properly, whereas those who breathe only superficially may survive, but they don't really nourish themselves.

One day, in order to help us to understand the importance of respiration, the Master Peter Deunov reminded us of the Biblical story of Jacob and the Angel. The Angel, having defeated Jacob, said, 'Let me go, for the day breaks.' But Jacob refused, saying, 'I will not let you go unless you bless me.' And the Master explained, 'This is what you must do with the air you breathe: you must embrace it and fill your lungs with it, and not let it go until it has surrendered all the blessings it contains.' Perhaps you thought that Jacob was simply doing violence to his adversary? No, he was acting out of zeal, out of spiritual fervour, and we should do the same. As long as the air has not given up all its blessings we must not let it go. This is the secret of all plenitude.

Chapter Six

RESPIRATION

I

The Effects of Respiration on Health

The science of breathing has been very highly developed in India for centuries, and the techniques used are often very complex. There is so much to this science, in fact, that it would take years, even centuries, to study it all. Thanks to their very extensive research, the ancient yogis and ascetics reached a deep understanding of the importance of respiration, not only in relation to physical vitality, but also in relation to the function of thought, for they came to see that all the rhythms of our organism were founded on the rhythms of the cosmos.

Now, don't think that I am advising you to launch into complicated breathing exercises, for I am not. On the contrary: you are not Indian yogis and if you are not very sensible and careful, you could become unbalanced and injure your health, as so many others have done before you.

The breathing exercises that we practise here, in our School, are very simple:

1. Begin by closing your left nostril and breathing in deeply through the right nostril, while counting to four.

2. Hold your breath to the count of sixteen.

3. Close your right nostril and breathe out through the left nostril to the count of eight.

Then you begin again, starting with the right nostril closed:

4. Breathe in through the left nostril to the count of four.

5. Hold your breath to the count of sixteen.

6. Breathe out through the right nostril to the count of eight.

Do this six times for each nostril.

Once the exercise has become easy for you, you can double the time of each movement, counting eight, thirty-two and sixteen, but I don't advise you to go any further than that.

Respiration has a role of paramount importance in the life of a spiritualist; this is why you must organize your daily programme so as to do your breathing exercises in the morning, on an empty stomach. It is not the same thing at all if you do them after breakfast, for the movement of the lungs is hampered. In fact, you can injure yourself by doing breathing exercises after a meal: they should always be done on an empty stomach or at least four or five hours after eating.

I should add that, when you take a deep breath with both nostrils, you must never inhale too rapidly; always inhale slowly and steadily. When you breathe out, on the other hand, you can expel the air rapidly and forcefully.

Breathe slowly and rhythmically, focusing all your attention on the air entering your lungs. Think of the elements that it contains and the good they will do your health. Perhaps some of you will object that you have been doing breathing exercises every day for years and that they have never done you any good. Well, in the first place, how can you be sure that they have not done you any good? Your health may not be perfect, but what would it have been like if you had not done these exercises? And secondly, are you sure that you were really concentrating on the healing you wanted from them while you were doing them? Didn't your thoughts often wander to the shopping expedition you were planning for that afternoon or to your latest argument with your wife or your boss? If your attention wanders, of course, you cannot expect them to do you much good! During your breathing exercises, all the cares and concerns of your daily life must be put aside; nothing must be allowed to distract you: all your thoughts and all your faith must be centred on the work you are doing. Faith is a divine sentiment which awakens unsuspected powers of thought and action; this is why it is at the root of all healing. Even if it is not actually your faith that heals you, it is still an essential condition for healing to occur.

Regular breathing exercises improve one's health. Each individual has his own method and his own rhythm which he must find by listening to his inner doctor. Yes, for each one of us has his own doctor within him, and those who don't listen to him will be obliged to listen, one day, to an external doctor! Listen to your inner doctor; he will show you how to breathe, how often and at what moments of the day to do these exercises, for you are all different and you must all find your own particular rhythm.

And speaking of doctors, it would be a good thing if they took care of people before they fell ill, if only to teach them how to breathe correctly. As a matter of fact, the doctors of the future will not tend the sick. Does that astonish you? It is because their task will be to teach people who are fit and well how to stay well, whereas, today, most of their work consists in trying to glue the pieces back together again... and they don't always succeed! Deep breathing is a very potent remedy, both as a preventive and as a curative, and if you do have to take medication, it will be all the more effective if you also breathe deeply and consciously.

When you draw air into the depths of your lungs, do so in the conscious conviction that you are receiving divine blessings with every breath you inhale. For many of you, all this is too new for it to come easily: you have difficulty in believing that God has put all the elements necessary to your health into the air you breathe. And yet it is so, and you must be convinced of it and make an effort to absorb them. You will ask, 'How can I do that?' It is very simple: you only have to think, as you breathe, that you are absorbing the elements you need, calcium, iodine, magnesium, etc. Your body knows very well what it needs; it has a whole team of very competent chemists at its service, and they know how to get what you need from the air. Of course, this will certainly not prevent you from having to buy certain medicines from the pharmacy, but you will need less of them if you learn how to get the elements you need by breathing. The only creature on earth capable of breathing consciously – for the moment, at any rate – is man: this is why man is said to be a living soul. So, try to be conscious that, when you breathe, you are absorbing divine life.

The divine life, the precious quintessence contained in the air around us, is known to Indian yogis as prâna. Prâna is at the root of all the energies of the cosmos and it is in the air in greatest abundance at sunrise. When we consciously draw in air through our nostrils, we set in motion the factories in our bodies whose task is to extract this quintessence and, once it has been extracted from the air, it circulates throughout our nervous system. In their studies of the human nervous system, the yogis and Sages of India found that this subtle quintessence, prâna, travels like fire through the network of nerves that run down either side of the spine. Just as the blood flows through the arteries, veins and capillaries, this extremely subtle fluidic energy, prâna, flows through the nervous system and nourishes and enhances our vitality, emotional balance and mental clarity. But, of course, one has to have a great deal of practice before being able to extract the prâna from the air.

Breathing is also very important for the functioning of the brain. It is good to read, study and meditate, but you must realize that the functioning of the brain depends on the rest of the body and, in particular, on the lungs. To be sure, the lungs do not act directly on the brain, but they have a very important role to play in purifying the blood and, when the blood is pure, it irrigates the brain and supplies it with elements which facilitate its work of understanding or meditation.

You should get into the habit, also, of taking a few deep breaths, several times a day, while placing your left hand flat on your solar plexus with the right hand over it. As you do this you should be able to feel your diaphragm expanding and contracting. The way in which you breathe affects your circulation and it is vitally important for all the organs of your body to give your circulation the best possible conditions.

And while we are on the subject of the diaphragm, you should know that it, too, has an important role to play in respiration. As you breathe in, the lungs expand and the diaphragm is pushed down, and as you breathe out, the lungs contract and the diaphragm moves up again. Certain illnesses of the digestive system or the lungs are due to a displacement or contraction of the diaphragm which is a very powerful muscle and which should always be relaxed and flexible.

Also, when you are doing breathing exercises, you must be careful to sit with your backbone as straight as possible. The spine plays an extremely important role in maintaining good health: everything depends on it; all kinds of disorders, both physical and psychic, can be caused by a deviation of the spinal column!

When we do our gymnastics here, every day, you must try to synchronize your breathing with the movements. Breathe in when you raise your arms, hold your breath for a moment, and breathe out only when you bend down: inhale on the upward movement and exhale on the downward movement. If you coordinate your breathing properly with the movements of the gymnastics, it will help you to

understand their significance and to get much more
out of them.[1]

One can also use deep breathing to ease certain
uncomfortable situations. Suppose, for instance,
that my room is cold and I have no means of
heating it: I take a deep breath and hold it for as
long as possible; in this way I send the warm blood
from the centre of my body out to the periphery.
Its warmth combats and protects me from the cold
outside. When you get into the habit of doing
breathing exercises you will find that your health,
your emotional balance, your clarity of thought
and even your will-power are enhanced. Try it: if
you have to lift something heavy it will be less of
an effort if you start by taking a deep breath. And if
you are upset, why not ask your lungs to help you?
That is what they are there for! Breathe deeply for
two or three minutes and you will find that you will
be quite calm again. It is normal to need help from
time to time, but why do you always have to look
for it on the outside when it is there, inside you?

You must learn to breathe consciously, that
is to say, to associate thought and respiration
and, thereby, awaken the forces dormant in the
subconscious. Deep breathing, when it is done
consciously, brings untold blessings for one's
intellectual, emotional and physical life and you

---

[1] See *A New Earth,* C.W. 13, Appendix.

should be able to see its beneficial effects not only on your brain but also in your soul and in all your faculties; it is an important factor in every aspect of life. Never neglect the question of respiration.

In all the minor events of everyday life, in all your relations with others, remember to breathe deeply: it will help you to remain in control of yourself. Before an interview, for example, if you want to ensure that a discussion will not degenerate into a quarrel, or before scolding or punishing a child, remember to cleanse yourself of everything that is upsetting you by taking a deep breath: your thoughts will become lighter and more luminous.

Study yourselves and observe how, when you are in pain or on the verge of giving way to anger or sensuality, you begin to pant, your breathing becomes shallow and irregular. Irregular breathing arouses negative forces. In fact, you only have to breathe fast and irregularly for five minutes and you will trigger negative forces within... and vice versa.

Have you noticed how a person's breathing becomes slower when they are asleep? Yes, because when you are asleep, you are inactive, so you burn up very little fuel and need very little air to stimulate combustion. When you are awake, on the other hand, particularly when you are very active, your breathing rate increases because you use up more fuel. It is thanks to his lungs that

man can expend a great deal of energy without
endangering his life. If he did not breathe, he
would not get the air he needs from the atmosphere
to replenish his energies and he would melt away
like a lighted candle. This is why I keep telling
you that those who insist that they are capable of
indulging in every kind of sexual effervescence
without exhausting their reserves, are blind and
ignorant. The rhythm of their breathing during
these moments of ferment proves, on the contrary,
that they involve a formidable expenditure of
energy.

The centres concerned with love are located
in the rear of the brain: above is the centre of the
love of family and friends and the capacity to
exchange and communicate with other human
beings, and below this, in the cerebellum, is the
centre of sexual love. If this lower centre receives
too strong an influx of blood, you feel the urge to
give free rein to your sensuality, but it is possible
to resist the urge by breathing deeply; after only a
few minutes you will find that you can behave in a
happier, more beneficial way.

Good breathing habits can also make our
exchanges with other people more harmonious.
Take a practical example: when people meet each
other they shake hands; with some people, their
handshake is warm and firm and shows that they
appreciate you, with others it is flabby; some shake

your hand carelessly, showing that the gesture does not mean much to them, others crush your fingers to a pulp! But what is important is that, when you shake hands with someone, a current should pass between you, otherwise there is no point in it. If you don't breathe deeply as you should, you will be incapable of shaking someone's hand properly. Before shaking hands with your friends or before going in to their house, take a deep breath (discreetly, of course); in this way your encounter with them will be harmonious.

You are given all kinds of exercises, here, and you must put them into practice. They will strengthen you and enable you to contend with your problems; and in all of them, what counts is the degree of attention and concentration that you bring to them; I have so often seen this to be true!

II

How to Melt into the Harmony of the Cosmos

Inhalation and exhalation, the ebb and flow of the movement by which we alternately fill and empty our lungs: this is what makes us alive. And it is a universal law; everything in nature breathes: animals, plants and even the earth itself. Yes, the earth is alive, so it too needs to breathe in and out. To be sure, it does not breathe exactly as we do, eighteen times a minute. The rhythm of the earth's breathing stretches over so many years that it is imperceptible to us. But it, too, dilates and contracts, its dimensions are never absolutely stable. In fact, it is possible that volcanic eruptions, ruptures of the earth's crust and many other phenomena are due to this expansion and contraction. The earth is alive and it breathes; the stars, too, breathe. Yes, they breathe in and out and their respiration is felt by us, here, on earth, as an influence.

I repeat: everything breathes, trees, the oceans, even stones. You will say, 'But you can't talk of breathing unless it involves lungs.' Why not? Life does not necessarily need to use the same organs in order to accomplish the same functions. Look at a tree, for instance: it has neither lungs nor stomach, neither liver nor intestines, and yet it breathes, nourishes itself, assimilates and reproduces! And it often lives a great deal longer than human beings! It can survive extremely severe weather conditions and produce sweet-scented flowers and fruits, whereas man, for all his intelligence, is so fragile that the slightest thing can destroy him.

By studying respiration and its relationship to the rhythms of the universe, Initiates have found that, in order to communicate with a particular region of the spiritual world, man has to choose the appropriate rhythm, make it his own and use it as a key to establish contact, exactly as one can tune a radio to a particular station if one knows the right wavelength. The wavelength is an essential factor in making contact with a particular broadcasting station and the same is true of breathing: you have to know what rhythm to adjust to, in order to make contact with a particular region of the universe.

In this way, respiration can unravel great mysteries for you, but only if you accompany it with some mental work. As you breathe out, think that you are expanding to the very outer limits of the universe and then, as you breathe in again, you contract and withdraw into yourself, into your ego, that imperceptible point at the centre of an infinite circle. Again you expand, and again you contract... In this way you discover the movement of ebb and flow which is the key to all the rhythms of the universe and, when you become conscious of this movement within your own being, you enter into the harmony of the cosmos and establish an exchange between yourself and the universe, for, as you breathe in, you inhale elements from space and, as you breathe out, you project, in return, something of your own heart and soul.

He who knows how to harmonize his being with the respiration of the cosmos enters into the sphere of divine consciousness. But so many of you are still very far from understanding the spiritual dimension of respiration! If you were sensitive to that dimension, you would work all your lives long to breathe in the strength and light of God and breathe out that light again to the whole world. For to breathe out is also this: to distribute the light of God that one has drawn into oneself.

To breathe in and breathe out... breathe in and breathe out... in and out... There is a link between respiration and every manifestation of the spiritual life. Meditation is a respiration; prayer is a respiration; ecstasy is a respiration; every form of communication with Heaven is a respiration, and your physical breathing reveals the intensity of that exchange. When you are in communion with Heaven you breathe deeply, as when you embrace your beloved.

Nature has placed keys to these mysteries in all kinds of places, and it is certain that, if philosophers practised respiration consciously, they would find the answers to many problems which are enigmas to them today. They continue to argue and write books about these things, but they have not understood them. The capacity for thought, in fact, is linked to respiration. If someone does not breathe properly, his mind becomes clouded.

He who has understood the profound significance of respiration gradually begins to sense that his own breathing melts into that of God. For God also breathes: He exhales and the world appears; He inhales and the world disappears. Of course, God's inhalations and exhalations take billions upon billions of years. The Hindu Sacred Scriptures speak of this: they tell us that, one day, God will breathe in and the universe will be swallowed up and dissolve into non-being. And then, once more, God will breathe out and a new creation will appear, to last, in its turn, for billions of years. The rhythm of God's breathing, as it manifests itself through man, is very rapid, but as it manifests itself in the cosmos, it is very, very slow. The slower our breathing, therefore, the nearer we come to the rhythm of God's breathing.

Now, one of the very best exercises you can do – and I advise you to get into the habit of doing it every day, several times a day – is to breathe light. Pick a quiet spot where no one will disturb you, sit down in a comfortable position and breathe: imagine that you are inhaling cosmic light, the light that is even subtler, infinitely subtler, than sunlight; that intangible, invisible, quintessential light that permeates all creation. Let this light soak into the depths of your being and flow through all your cells, all the organs of your body. Then, as you breathe out, draw it up and project it outwards to enlighten, illuminate and help every single creature in the world. This is a truly extraordinary exercise for, in the terms of the Cabbalah, you become the letter Aleph. Aleph, the first letter of the Hebrew alphabet symbolizes him who reaches up to receive light from Heaven with one hand and distributes it, with the other hand, to all human beings. You cannot become Aleph if you think only of yourself, if you keep it all for yourself. Aleph is he whose only concern is to give, to warm, enlighten and vivify others, without a thought for himself. He is a creator, a saviour of mankind, a son of God.

He who learns to breathe consciously develops a clearer mind, a warmer heart and a stronger will; he also prepares better conditions for his future incarnations. Yes, because, by his conscious participation in what he is doing, he becomes attuned to very highly advanced entities; they are attracted to him, a bond is created and these luminous entities are willing to come and work in him so that, one day, when he leaves this earth, he will come face to face with these 'friends and allies' with whom he has been learning to work on earth. Never forget that your body is a society whose members make a constant effort to maintain unity. At the moment, you still do not know your associates who live within you but, when you go to the next world, you will not only meet them and find out that they were your friends and that you lived in the same house together, but that you are going to be associates again, in your next incarnation. This is a very important question, and anyone who wants to manifest himself properly and accomplish the divine mission for which he has been sent to earth, must be aware of it.

And now, let's look at another question that you have never thought about: when we inhale, we take oxygen from the atmosphere, and it is this that keeps us alive; whereas, when we breathe out, we reject carbon dioxide and other pollutants. Everybody knows this and thinks that that is the

end of it, that there is nothing they can do about
it. But that is not so: why should man continue
to extract pure, life-giving elements from the
universe and give back only poison and impurities?
To be sure, as long as he has not attained a life
of inner purity, this state of affairs will continue,
but once he begins to think, feel and act divinely,
he will no longer pollute the atmosphere with his
impurities. He will breathe in pure life and he will
breathe out pure life. You may think that this is
impossible. I assure you: it is perfectly possible.
There have been saints and Initiates of such purity
that everything that came from them, all their
exhalations, embalmed the air around them. The
divine life that entered them was unsullied by any
impurity or evil so that, when they gave it back
to the world, it was still as limpid, luminous and
beneficial as when they had received it.

If you study the first letter of the Hebrew
alphabet, Aleph א , you will understand that it is
a symbol of exchange, of a giving and receiving.
You receive light and you give light to others; you
receive purity and you give purity; you receive love
and you give love. This is why Jesus could say, 'I
am Aleph', for he is the only one who irradiates a
light as pure as that he receives.

I realize that I am leading you into regions
that are virtually inaccessible, but if your ideal
is to give back light, the divine light and purity

that you yourself have received, this is already a preparation for the day when whatever you project, all your emanations, will be pure light. And there is only one way to achieve this ideal: to devote all your work to propagating the idea of brotherhood throughout the world, to work for the coming of the Kingdom of God and His Righteousness on earth. Only then will the air you breathe out be a life-giving breath.

Chapter Seven

NUTRITION ON THE DIFFERENT PLANES

You must all have observed, at one time or another, that when you have eaten well, you are ready to see the beauty of life, but that when you have nothing to eat, even life seems to lose all meaning for you. But then, I wonder: have you ever actually been in a situation where you had nothing to eat? No, most of you have never experienced that and, in that case, you cannot really understand, you cannot feel with your whole being, that nutrition is the foundation of life.

If, as I say, nutrition is the foundation of life, it is important to pay attention to what one eats. I am not going to go into details about this; more and more books about healthy eating and a balanced diet are available today. But the aspect that has always interested me, and which I shall continue to insist on, is the way we eat. Nutrition is a very vast subject: the whole question is how to nourish oneself. Naturally, I recommend a

healthy, vegetarian diet,[1] no alcohol or foods that
have been chemically processed and, above all,
nothing in excess. Doctors have recently sounded
the alarm because people eat too much sugar,
too much salt and too much fat. One of the first
qualities to acquire is prudence, moderation, and
this is why I cannot endorse the attitude of those
who exaggerate the importance of diet. Some say
that one should only eat cereals, others want us
to eat nothing but fruit, etc., and we should never
touch a drop of wine, tea or coffee! No, that is
exaggerated. You have to be reasonable, that's
all. A little wine occasionally cannot do anyone
any harm unless, of course, his health is already
heavily compromised. As for coffee, it has a
favourable effect on the solar plexus and, if you
drink a cup in the morning before your meditation,
you will feel stimulated.

It is up to each person to decide what he needs
according to his health and his own particular
temperament. It is not really my role to give you
detailed advice on this score; there are others
who are better qualified to do so. More and more
people, even in the Brotherhood, are studying the
question, and that is good: it is important. But

---

[1] A vegetarian diet which excludes only meat and meat
products, but allows eggs, dairy products and even fish. See *The
Yoga of Nutrition*, Izvor 204, chap. 5: 'Choosing Your Food'.

to my mind, the most important is to realize that nutrition does not apply only to the physical body. True, the survival of the physical body depends on having enough food, but the heart, mind, soul and spirit also need food and it is because human beings don't know this, that they no longer know the meaning of life.

Life is nothing more than an endless exchange between the universe and the tiny atoms that we represent. Cosmic life flows into man who impregnates it with his own emanations before sending it back into the universe. Once again, he absorbs this life and, once again, he returns it. And it is this ongoing exchange between man and the universe that we call nutrition, that we call respiration and that we also call love. Life is an exchange between two worlds, and he who refuses all exchange dies. We have to exchange with the earth in order to live on the physical plane; we have to exchange with water in order to live on the astral plane, the plane of the heart; we have to exchange with air in order to live on the mental plane, the plane of the mind, and we have to exchange with heat and light in order to live on the plane of our soul and spirit.

But I wonder if you can have any conception of what the cosmic dimension of nutrition represents, of the fact that human beings must seek the nourishment needed by their different bodies in different regions of the universe. Try to understand this and you will begin to sense that the universe is one immense symphony.

You must no longer envisage nourishment as something that applies exclusively to the physical plane. To eat is not enough. The fact that so many people who eat two, three or four times a day still complain of feeling empty and dissatisfied makes this very obvious.

Nutrition is of prime importance. Yes, but nutrition on every level: an exchange not only with the more material but also with the subtler levels of the universe. The only thing is that, for this exchange to take place, the channels of communication must be clear. If they are clogged up nothing can get through, your energies cannot circulate and this leads to problems. It is a question of keeping your pipes and conduits clean: if they are blocked up you must unblock them. How? By purification. When the obstruction is in your physical body, you deal with it by fasting and a purge or an enema, and when it is on the psychic level, you can get rid of it by purification.

Prayer, meditation and ecstasy are all forms of nourishment. Thanks to them you enjoy a celestial food, ambrosia, the food of immortality. This is an immaterial food but, for alchemists who knew it as the Elixir of Everlasting Life, it also existed on the physical plane. Yes, it is true: it does exist on the physical plane and it is diffused throughout nature by the sun. If we attend the sunrise every day, during spring and summer, it is in order to drink in this ambrosia, this quintessence of life that the sun distributes to every region of the universe and of which the rocks, plants and animals, as well as human beings, all receive some particles. But if all living creatures receive these particles unconsciously, men must learn to extract them consciously from this fiery fluid, the light of the sun.

In the new civilization that is on the way, human beings will learn to nourish themselves with these subtle particles. I know that many of you will be surprised to hear this, and yet this new way of nourishing oneself is in the natural order of things. We must not be content only with the denser kinds of physical nourishment, for it creates too much waste which encumbers and poisons our system. Whereas when we nourish ourselves with light there is no waste; light is the only thing that never creates waste because light is pure. When you burn wood or coal in your fireplace, you have to clean out the ashes before lighting it again, next day; and the same principle applies to your body: if you didn't evacuate the waste left over from what you eat and drink, you would die. Illness is caused by residues of waste in the body. Yes, illness can be

defined as an accumulation of matter that the body
has been unable to eliminate. Health, on the other
hand, is the result of transformations so subtle and
rapid that no impurities remain in the body.

When you have learned to absorb the pure
quintessence that is diffused by the sun you will
feel your health improving, your intelligence
becoming more lucid, your heart expanding and
your will becoming stronger. You will, perhaps,
say, 'Yes, but I have been contemplating the
sun for months and years without any signs of
improvement!' All that this means is that you have
not been doing it in the right way. Results depend
on the way in which we do things, not on the time
we spend doing them! Each time you manage to
take a few sips from the inexhaustible source of the
sun, you will feel substantial improvements taking
place within you.

Chapter Eight

HOW TO BECOME TIRELESS

How often one hears the words, 'I'm tired!' Yes, everybody is tired. And yet they still rush off in all directions and bustle about without a minute's pause. It is good to want to be active, but in order to remain active without tiring oneself out, one must know how to relax... not once or twice a day, but ten, fifteen, twenty times a day, if only for a minute at a time. As soon as you have a moment to spare, wherever you may be, instead of fretting at being kept waiting, take advantage of the occasion to recapture your peace and get back onto an even keel, and you will be all the readier to go back to your activities with renewed strength.

The thing that does more harm than anything else to contemporary man is the feverish pace, the continual strain under which he lives and which is so detrimental to his psychic health. Not only does this constant scramble make it impossible for a man's qualities to manifest themselves, but it also leads to all kinds of anomalies of behaviour.

As I sometimes say to people, 'You leave your 'taps' running day and night and, in the end, your reservoirs are empty, your nervous system is exhausted. If you would only think of turning off your taps for a few minutes, you would never be exhausted.'

From time to time you must deliberately become passive. Not just any kind of passivity, of course. The passivity I am speaking of is a state in which you should be able to recharge your batteries and, in order to do this you must remain in intelligent control, otherwise, instead of replenishing your heavenly energies, a passive attitude is liable to attract only negative currents. As a matter of fact, this is a very important question which affects every aspect of man's psychic life and which receptive beings, such as mediums, would do well to study. If one is not conscious and watchful, one attracts both good and bad elements and, unfortunately, more often the bad than the good! This is why it is important to learn to become conscious mediums, capable of being in a state of passivity without attracting anything negative.

If you want to become indefatigable you must learn to work with the two principles, masculine and feminine, emissive and receptive. It is not possible to be active all day long so, when it is time for a pause in your activity, put yourself consciously into a state of receptivity, taking care to keep in touch with Heaven, so as to attract only pure, luminous energies.

It is not easy to learn to economize energy. People are greedy but they are not economical. It is not necessarily selfish to be economical any more than it is always a proof of generosity to be prodigal: on the contrary, it is more often proof of a lack of discernment. Yes, you must learn to make the distinction: those who squander their energies and throw everything overboard are considered generous, but this is false: they may be imprudent, vain, stupid or whatever else you like, but not generous! In order to be truly generous one has to learn the art of being economical, otherwise, when you have squandered everything, what will you have left to give to others? And to be economical means to spend just the right amount and no more of each thing, at the right time and in the right place.

You don't think enough about adopting a passive attitude; you let yourselves get caught up in the fevered atmosphere that has now become normal and which is extremely detrimental to man's psychic equilibrium. From now on, you must take better care of your nervous system and give it a chance to relax from time to time. Take just a quarter of an hour each day – fifteen times one minute – in which to relax. You will see: it will not be a waste of time, on the contrary, you will gain a

lot from it. I have no doubt that many of you will
object, 'But I have so much to do!' I know that, but
you could still find the time to retreat into a quiet
room, to stretch out face down on a bed, or flat on
the floor, arms and legs relaxed, and let yourself
go as though you were sinking into an ocean of
light, and to remain motionless without thinking of
anything, for just one minute! If you did this you
would get up with your batteries recharged.

There, that is all; it is not much, but it is very
important. Use this method frequently and you
will see for yourself: you will be full of energy all
day long. Otherwise, even when you have nothing
to do, you will be tired. I am sure that you have
already experienced this: sometimes you have not
done anything and you are still tired; even after
three hours in a deck-chair, you are still exhausted!
Why? Because you have not thought of turning off
those inner taps and, however much you rest, your
strength trickles away to no purpose. And that is
a pity, because your fatigue causes you to neglect
the only activities that really matter.

In speaking about the need to relax, I have not
mentioned the more basic factors: obviously you
cannot be on top of your form if you don't eat and
sleep and breathe correctly. If you have not eaten
for a long time, you can relax as much as you like

but you will not replenish your strength that way. In recommending that you take the time to relax, I take it for granted that you breathe and eat and sleep as you should:[1] that is indispensable. But even if you have stored up a lot of energy in that way, you may lose it again much too quickly if you don't know how to recharge your batteries. Sleep, nourishment and breathing, therefore, are indispensable pre-conditions, whereas relaxation is a psychic means that will help you to distribute your energy evenly and adequately and to recharge your batteries when necessary.

To be sure, there are some yogis and Initiates who have achieved such a degree of mastery over their thought that, even without eating or drinking or sleeping, they are able to maintain an extremely intense contact with the great reservoirs of cosmic forces, and receive tremendous strength which they transform into the energy they need for their physical bodies. This is possible; such beings do exist, but they are very few and far between; one has to be extraordinarily practised to attain this level and none of you have attained it yet.

So, as you see, I put each element in place, pointing out what is essential and what is not, what is possible and what is not, and it is up to you, now,

---

[1] For a fuller discussion of the question of sleep, see *A New Earth*, C.W. 13, chap. 2: 'Preparing for sleep'.

to understand me and apply correctly the methods
I explain to you.

And now let me add, once again, that the real
key to being able to sustain a high level of activity
in the best possible conditions is to learn to work
with love. For it is love that strengthens, vivifies
and resuscitates. Yes: love! When this love is not
present, when a man works only for money, to earn
his living, the results are not what they should be.
To be sure, he earns a few pennies but his nerves
and his general health suffer. You can work for
hours with love and not feel the least bit tired; but
if you work, even if only for a few minutes, without
love, in a spirit of anger and revolt, everything
starts to seize up inside you and you will end up
flat on your back. There are ideologies at work in
the world today which attempt to spread a spirit of
revolt and discontent amongst all the workers in the
world, and which are extraordinarily successful.
Yes, because they are setting sparks to tinder! It
is very easy: if you decide to spread the spirit of
revolt you are bound to succeed. But try telling
people that discontent is detrimental to themselves
and that they should start to work with love, and
you will get nowhere. Men are not mature enough
to understand where their true interest lies.

It is important to understand the power and the
efficacy of love. Whatever you do, do it with love,
or don't do it at all! Whatever you do without love

can only fatigue and poison you, and then you need not be surprised to find yourself ill with exhaustion. Do everything with love! Try it; it is entirely up to you. Someone asked me, one day, how to become tireless, and this is what I told them: 'I can certainly give you the secret, but will you be able to apply it? The secret is to feel a great deal of love for everything you do, for it is love that awakens all man's latent powers.'

You are in a divine School in which you are learning to reconstruct yourselves. You have still not fully grasped how important this task is, but you should be happy to know that, at last, you have the prospect of being in a position to put your life back onto the right track.

Chapter Nine

CULTIVATE AN ATTITUDE
OF CONTENTMENT

One rarely hears someone talking about the importance of being contented and satisfied. Very few people realize how terribly destructive it is always to be dissatisfied with everything and everyone and to introduce a climate of disharmony wherever one goes. And what is even more serious is the modern tendency to consider contentment to be a sign of unintelligence and lack of sophistication, whereas an attitude of dissatisfaction is seen as a sign of intelligence.

To be sure, if you only pretend to be dissatisfied from time to time, in order to impress people, it will not do too much harm, but if dissatisfaction really takes root in you the results could be disastrous, and you would do well to take precautions against such an occurrence. It is important to analyse the causes of a deep-seated sense of dissatisfaction, and they are often to be found either in a faulty reasoning process or in defects in one's education.

On the intellectual level, a prolonged attitude of discontent, whether conscious or unconscious,

444

44

4444

44

is always corrosive. Someone who always has some complaint to make against the Lord, against life or against mankind in general, must be warned that this is a very pernicious attitude and that it will lead him to make all kinds of mistakes. As he cannot prevent his feelings from showing, the face of a discontented man will be sombre and lacklustre, his eyes will have no light in them, his voice will be harsh and his gestures brusque... and all this will make him very unattractive to others. Although it is true that people tend to see discontent as a sign of intelligence, this does not prevent them from finding the discontented very difficult to put up with and from keeping well away from them! How can anyone take pleasure in associating with those who never stop grumbling and poisoning the atmosphere with their complaints and recriminations? Discontent is a black smoke which invades a man's soul, and he who entertains it ends by destroying himself. Obviously, no one expects you to be full of unwavering good humour and joy from one day to the next. Good humour is often simply the expression of a particular type of temperament and nothing is more difficult to change than one's temperament. Nevertheless, it is possible, by means of thought, love and will-power, to modify one's inner attitudes.

If people were really honest and lucid they would recognize that the positive aspects of life are always greater in both quantity and quality. Let me give you a very simple example: here, on the Riviera, fine days far outnumber the rainy days, but at the first sign of a shower, you all complain about the bad weather; you forget all the weeks of beautiful weather we have had! Yes, and this is how people react in every domain. To be discontented is to admit that one refuses to have a clear, objective view of reality. You must at least have the honesty to see both sides.

Someone who is always satisfied and optimistic is not entirely justified either, but to fly into a rage because someone says something that offends you, because something has cost you more than you thought it would or because your soup is too salty or your newspaper has disappeared, and to react to these minor inconveniences as though they were world-shaking disasters, creates an inner state that is self-destructive. Try, from now on, to weigh all the little irritations of everyday life against the fact that you have arms and legs that enable you to do all kinds of wonderful things; that you have eyes and ears, a mouth and a nose with which to see and hear, to feel, breathe, taste, speak and admire... And then, too, you have a profession, a house and friends. Are you going to forget all these priceless treasures and disrupt the life of your family and of society for the sake of a few minor vexations? If so, it only shows how unintelligent you are.

Yes, use the method of comparison: compare the little inconveniences of life with the great gifts that Providence has bestowed on you with such generosity, and draw your own conclusions. All too often we do just the opposite: we compare the little we have with what our neighbours have: 'Look at him, he's got a car and I've only got a bike!' or, 'She's got real diamonds and I've only got a string of false pearls!' It is very bad to make comparisons of this kind. If you must make comparisons, why not see how many advantages you have compared to so many people who are poor, unhappy or ill? The constant ingratitude and discontent of men shows a distinct lack of intelligence: instead of recognizing all the blessings that Heaven showers on them they see everything as a reason to lose their faith, love and gratitude.

You will tell me that you have good cause to be unhappy; that at every turn you meet with failure; that your future prospects are dismal, etc. The truth is, though, that no two days are alike; if the sun was hidden by the clouds today, tomorrow you will see it rising and everything will smile on you once more. 'That's all very well', some of you may say: 'But I'm already old. What have I got to look forward to?' Don't you know that, one day, you will come back to earth again as a child, and that, rich with your past experience, you will begin a new life with every hope of a bright future?

There is an answer to every objection that can be raised by sadness and discouragement, but it implies that you agree to look at things from a different point of view and change the way you reason. Pause for an instant to reflect on each event or situation and try to see both aspects, the negative and the positive. It is no good living in a fool's paradise and saying that everything is wonderful, but you must also refuse to dwell only on the dark side of life. You think, 'I know all that!' Well, if you know it, do it! Observe your own behaviour and you will see that you often forget this rule and give way to discontent and pessimism. And then, not only are you incapable of thinking rationally, but you prevent your soul from blossoming and taking flight. This is how you destroy yourself spiritually and even physically.

Dissatisfaction is acceptable only if it is aimed at oneself. You must not be satisfied with yourself even if you achieve considerable spiritual progress. Why not? Because self-satisfaction can turn into vanity and smugness and put a stop to all progress, and then your striving for perfection would come to an end. Whereas a feeling of dissatisfaction with yourself will be a stimulus to work and improve. But in order to prevent this dissatisfaction from becoming a destructive obsession, you must counteract it by an attitude of satisfaction with others. This will protect you from a too negative attitude which could lead to real discouragement. Try to see beauty and goodness in others, especially in those who have contributed to the evolution of mankind by their genius or their virtues. In this way you will always have something to marvel at and will be in no danger of giving way to despair.

There have been musicians, poets and painters of genius who, in a fit of discouragement, have destroyed their own creations. This is simply because they were walled up in their solitude and incapable of seeing beyond themselves or of finding anything good in others; if they had been able to rejoice in the good to be found in others it would have protected them from turning their discouragement against themselves and their own creations. Initiates are not satisfied with themselves but they are very satisfied with the works of God and full of admiration for His servants. In this way they counteract the dissatisfaction caused by their own imperfections.

If someone finds that he is incapable of manifesting the qualities that he hoped to possess he must not give way to discouragement or revolt. Anger or discouragement, whether it be directed at himself, at others or at the Lord, is extremely destructive: he must try to be humbler; otherwise it means that his reasoning is at fault and that he is still subject to his own lower nature which has succeeded in taking advantage of favourable circumstances to gain control. It is as though Heaven had passed the word to certain beings or circumstances to afflict or insult him in some way to see how he would react. And the ensuing turmoil is proof enough that he was not ready for these trials. Well, even if this is the case, he must not let himself be depressed or discouraged, for this would mean that conceit had led him to grasp at things that were still beyond his reach, and if he does nothing to remedy the situation, he will end by destroying himself. It is legitimate to be sad, but only about other people's misfortunes or failures, not because of one's own unfulfilled desires or ambitions. Those who are often sad for these reasons must realize that they are not very highly evolved because their sadness has an inferior cause.

To sum up, let me say that there is a current of life and a current of death, and that the first step towards death is discontent. Yes, for if you are not careful, discontent turns to sorrow and sorrow turns to pain. Pain begins on the psychic plane, but it ends on the physical plane and, one day, it becomes illness, and illness leads to death. There are many different steps on the path from discontent to death, but the one inevitably leads to the other. Contentment, on the contrary, puts you squarely on the road to life. He who is contented is filled with gratitude to Heaven and lives in a state of peace; peace gives him strength; strength brings him fulfilment and he begins to taste the delights of eternal Life.

He who aspires to perfection, who asks the spirits of nature to help him in his work, must be grateful for all that he has and give something positive to others. From now on, learn to be contented, particularly with all the things that you have always scorned or neglected. Try to find at least one beautiful thing to marvel at every day and enshrine it in your heart and mind. If you thank the Lord every day, if you are pleased with whatever He gives you, the magic secret that will enable you to transform your life will be yours, and the luminous spirits of nature will gather round you to help you.

Books by Omraam Mikhaël Aïvanhov
(translated from the French)
Complete Works

Brochures:
New Presentation

Daily Meditations:
A thought for each day of the year

World Wide - Editor-Distributor
Editions PROSVETA S.A. - B.P. 12 - F- 83601 Fréjus Cedex (France)
Tel. (00 33) 04 94 19 33 33 - Fax (00 33) 04 94 19 33 34
Web: **www.prosveta.com**
e-mail: **international@prosveta.com**

Distributors

AUSTRALASIA
SURYOMA LTD - P.O. Box 2218 – Bowral – N.S.W. 2576 Australia
e-mail: info@suryoma.com – Tel. (61) 2 4872 3999 – fax (61) 2 4872 4022

AUSTRIA
HARMONIEQUELL VERSAND – A- 5302 Henndorf am Wallersee, Hof 37
Tel. / fax (43) 6214 7413 – e-mail: info@prosveta.at

BELGIUM & LUXEMBOURG
PROSVETA BENELUX – Liersesteenweg 154 B-2547 Lint
Tel (32) 3/455 41 75 – Fax (32) 3/454 24 25 – e-mail: prosveta@skynet.be
N.V. MAKLU Somersstraat 13-15 – B-2000 Antwerpen
Tel. (32) 3/231 29 00 – Fax (32) 3/233 26 59
VANDER S.A. – Av. des Volontaires 321 – B-1150 Bruxelles
Tél. (32)(0)2 732 35 32 – Fax. (32) (0)2 732 42 74 – e-mail: g.i.a@wol.be

BULGARIA
SVETOGLED – Bd Saborny 16 A, appt 11 – 9000 Varna
e-mail: svetgled@revolta.com – Tel/Fax: (359) 52 23 98 02

CANADA
PROSVETA Inc. – 3950, Albert Mines – Canton-de-Hatley (Qc), J0B 2C0
Tel. (819) 564-8212 – Fax. (819) 564-1823
in Canada, call toll free: 1-800-854-8212
e-mail: prosveta@prosveta-canada.com / www.prosveta-canada.com

COLUMBIA
PROSVETA – Calle 149 N° 24 B - 20 – Bogotá
Tel. (57) 1 614 88 28 – Fax (57) 1 633 58 03 – Mobile (57) 310 2 35 74 55
e-mail: kalagiya@tutopia.com

CYPRUS
THE SOLAR CIVILISATION BOOKSHOP – BOOKBINDING
73 D Kallipoleos Avenue - Lycavitos – P. O. Box 24947, 1355 – Nicosia
e-mail: cypapach@cytanet.com.cy – Tel / Fax 00357-22-377503

CZECH REPUBLIC
PROSVETA – Ant. Sovy 18, –České Budejovice 370 05
Tel / Fax: (420) 38-53 10 227 – e-mail: prosveta@iol.cz

GERMANY
PROSVETA Deutschland – Heerstrasse 55 – 78628 Rottweil
Tel. (49) 741-46551 – Fax. (49) 741-46552 – e-mail: prosveta.de@t-online.de

GREAT BRITAIN – IRELAND
PROSVETA – The Doves Nest, Duddleswell Uckfield, – East Sussex TN 22 3JJ
Tel. (44) (01825) 712988 - Fax (44) (01825) 713386
e-mail: prosveta@pavilion.co.uk

GREECE
RAOMRON – D. RAGOUSSIS
3, rue A. Papamdreou – C.P. 16675 – Glifada - Athenes
Tel / Fax: (010) 9681127 – e-mail: raomron@hol.gr

HAITI
PROSVETA – DÉPÔT – B.P. 115, Jacmel, Haiti (W.I.)
Tel./ Fax (509) 288-3319
e-mail: haiti@prosveta.com

HOLLAND
STICHTING PROSVETA NEDERLAND
Zeestraat 50 – 2042 LC Zandvoort
Tel. (31) 33 25 345 75 – Fax. (31) 33 25 803 20
e-mail: prosveta@worldonline.nl

ISRAEL
Zohar, P. B. 1046, Netanya 42110
e-mail: zohar7@012.net.il

ITALY
PROSVETA Coop. a r.l. – Casella Postale 55 – 06068 Tavernelle (PG)
Tel. (39) 075-835 84 98 – Fax (39) 075-835 97 12
e-mail: prosveta@tin.it

LIBAN
PROSVETA LIBAN – P.O. Box 90-995
Jdeidet-el-Metn, Beirut – Tel. (03) 448560
e-mail: prosveta_lb@terra.net.lb

NORWAY
PROSVETA NORDEN – Postboks 318, N-1502 Moss
Tel. (47) 69 26 51 40 – Fax (47) 69 25 06 76
e-mail: prosnor@online.no

PORTUGAL & BRAZIL
EDIÇÕES PROSVETA
Rua Passos Manuel, n° 20 – 3ᵉ E, P 1150 – 260 Lisboa
Tel. (351) (21) 354 07 64 – Fax (351) (21) 798 60 31
e-mail : prosvetapt@hotmail.com
PUBLICAÇÕES EUROPA-AMERICA Ltd
Est Lisboa-Sintra KM 14 – 2726 Mem Martins Codex

ROMANIA
ANTAR – Str. N. Constantinescu 10 - Bloc 16A - sc A - Apt. 9,
Sector 1 – 71253 Bucarest
Tel. 004021-231 28 78 - Tel./ Fax 004021-231 37 19
e-mail : antared@pcnet.ro

RUSSIA
EDITIONS PROSVETA
143 964 Moskovskaya oblast, g. Reutov – 4, post/box 4
Tel./ Fax. (095) 525 18 17 – Tél. (095) 795 70 74
e-mail: prosveta@online.ru

SPAIN
ASOCIACIÓN PROSVETA ESPAÑOLA – C/ Ausias March n° 23 Ático
SP-08010 Barcelona – Tel (34) (93) 412 31 85 - Fax (34) (93) 318 89 01
aprosveta@prosveta.es

UNITED STATES
PROSVETA US Dist.
PO Box 2125 – Canyon Country CA 91386
Tél. (661)252-1751 – Fax. (661) 252-9090
e-mail: prosveta_usa@earthlink.net / www.prosveta-usa.com

SWITZERLAND
PROSVETA Société Coopérative
Ch. de la Céramone 3A – CH - 1808 Les Monts-de-Corsier
Tél. (41) 21 921 92 18 – Fax. (41) 21 922 92 04
e-mail: prosveta@swissonline.ch

VENEZUELA
PROSVETA VENEZUELA C. A. – Calle Madrid
Edificio La Trinidad – Las Mercedes – Caracas D.F.
Tel. (58) 414 22 36 748 – e-mail : betty_mramirez@hotmail.com

The aim of the Universal White Brotherhood association
is the study and practice of the Teaching
of Master Omraam Mikhaël Aïvanhov,
published and distributed
by Prosveta.
All enquiries about the association should be addressed to:
Universal White Brotherhood
The Doves Nest, Duddleswell, Uckfield
East Sussex TN22 3JJ, GREAT BRITAIN
Tel: (44) (0)1825 712150 – Fax: (44) (0)1825 713386
E-mail: uwb@pavilion.co.uk

Printed in September 2004
by DUMAS-TITOULET Imprimeurs
42004 Saint-Etienne – France

Dépôt légal : Septembre 2004
Imprimeur : 41048B
1er dépôt légal dans la même collection: 1988